4.95

F.952
10

OUR MAN in HEAVEN

AN EXPOSITION OF THE EPISTLE TO THE HEBREWS

EDWARD FUDGE

BAKER BOOK HOUSE
Grand Rapids, Michigan

PHOTOLITHOPRINTED BY CUSHING - MALLOY, INC.
ANN ARBOR, MICHIGAN, UNITED STATES OF AMERICA
1974

DEDICATED

TO

THE MEMORY OF

BENJAMIN LEE FUDGE

———

father in the flesh
brother in the faith
esteemed teacher
dear friend

———

"These all died in faith, not having received the promises, but having seen them afar off, and were persuaded of them, and embraced them, and confessed that they were strangers and pilgrims on the earth. . . . Wherefore God is not ashamed to be called their God: for he hath prepared for them a city."

FOREWORD

"OUR MAN IN HEAVEN" sums up very aptly the central emphasis of the Letter to the Hebrews. The human family has in the presence of God an acceptable Representative — acceptable because He is most authentically one with ourselves, partaker of our flesh and blood, and acceptable too because He is *persona gratissima* with God, being the Son through whom God has spoken His final and perfect word to mankind.

Our Lord's present ministry on His people's behalf "in matters for which they are responsible to God" guarantees for them an inexhaustible supply of grace and power to cope with all the troubles and temptations that are inseparable from present life on earth. Provision to match the need of the moment comes the more opportunely from One who, when on earth, was spared none of these troubles and temptations, but endured them all and triumphed over them.

Next, our Lord's presence before God on our behalf guarantees for us also free access before God. Since God welcomes Him as our Representative, He welcomes by the same token those whom our Lord represents. Both now and hereafter the way into the heavenly sanctuary stands open through Him for those who are united with Him by faith. He who is the source of our present help is also the ground of our eternal hope.

Again, our Lord now ministers as our Representative in the presence of God because He has blazed a trail thither along which He now calls us to follow Him.

The first readers of this Letter were reluctant to leave the familiar securities of their ancestral pattern of religious life for the hazardous adventure of following One who set such little store by His own personal security. But if men and women in the first century A. D. had not been willing to do this very thing — to obey the injunction "Let us go forth" — there would have been no future for the Christian cause on earth. It is equally necessary for us 1900 years later to be ready to leave *our* familiar securities and follow Him who is still calling His people along the unpredictable trail of faith. To know this by experience is also involved in understanding what is meant by having "our Man in heaven."

It is a pleasure to commend Mr. Fudge's exposition of the Letter to the Hebrews. A superficial perusal of the Letter may suggest that it has little relevance to readers today. A more careful study reveals that its message is astonishingly up-to-date, speaking directly to the conditions of Christian existence in this uncertain world. I hope that, with the help of Mr. Fudge's study, many readers will grasp the message of the Letter and learn to live by it.

Manchester, England   F. F. BRUCE
November 1972

CONTENTS

INTRODUCTION

Authorship

At the end of the second century, opinion was divided regarding the authorship of the Epistle to the Hebrews. Clement of Alexandria believed that Paul wrote the epistle in Hebrew and that Luke translated it into Greek. Origen thought that someone familiar with Paul's teachings wrote Hebrews, but he added his now-famous remark that "who really wrote the letter is known to God alone." At Carthage, Tertullian suggested the name of Barnabas. Christians in Rome and in the West generally confessed that they did not know who wrote Hebrews. Archer points out that "none of the ancient authorities . . . entertained any doubt as to the *canonicity* (i.e. the divine inspiration) of the Epistle," however, and that "in any event the primary author . . . is God Himself, no matter which human instrument He used." In the days of the Reformation, Luther favored Apollos as the author and Calvin looked to Clement of Rome or possibly Luke.

Date of Writing

The date of this epistle is also uncertain. References to the Jewish order and the priestly functions seem clearly to involve the Levitical service of the Old Testament, not the distorted institutions of the first century after Christ. Nor can it be ascertained whether the calamity of A.D. 70 had befallen Jerusalem and Herod's Temple when our author wrote. Internal evidence is claimed for both positions. We must set a latest possible date before A.D. 96, for Clement of Rome wrote then and he quotes from the epistle quite freely. We can not have too early a date, for a few remarks in the epistle indicate that its first recipients were second-generation Christians (2:3-4; 13:7) and apparently not new converts themselves (5:12; 10:32-35).

Recipients

Beyond what has been stated we can know little of the recipients or their precise historical situation. So far as a general statement of affairs, most scholars would probably agree with Bernard that the epistle

> . . . evidently belongs to the last hour of transition and decision, when a large number of men, who were at once Jews and Christians, stood perplexed, agitated, and almost distracted, as they seemed to feel the ground parting beneath their feet, and hardly knew whether to throw themselves back on that which was receding, or forward on that to which they were called to cling. In an intense sympathy with this perplexity, and even anguish, prevailing in the Hebrew-Christian mind, and in an intense anxiety as to its issue, the Epistle was written; a living voice of power in a time of change and fear, yet a comprehensive exposition of the advancing course of revelation, and of the relation between its two great stages (pages 161-162).

Just what was involved in this crisis-time is not so clear, and regarding that there is a wide divergence of views.

In an article in *The Expository Times*, Bruce sums up recent views regarding the epistle's recipients. Candidates include the Christians of the Lycus Valley (Colossae, Laodicea), Jewish Christians in Ephesus, Hebrew converts in Rome who hesitated to declare themselves a part of the "illicit religion" of Christ rather than the "licit religion" (in the eyes of official Rome) of the Jews, Jewish Christians of Corinth, Jewish convert hotheads who had fled to Alexandria after the fall of Jerusalem, Hebrew Christians on Cyprus, and Palestinian Jewish Christians either before or after the destruction of A.D. 70. The Dead Sea

Scrolls evidence certain parallel interests between their authors and the recipients of Hebrews. Both are concerned with the position and role of angels, with certain Old Testament passages, with the priesthood and even with Melchizedek. This has led some scholars to posit a connection between the readers of our epistle and the Qumran community of the Scrolls, or, at least, between this epistle and converted Jewish priests.

In the midst of all this uncertainty, and with no real prospects of additional light on the subject, Filson believes "it is unfortunate that so much attention has been paid to questions of authorship, destination, place of writing and date," and that "the frustratingly inconclusive study of Hebrews should make it clear that we cannot find certain answers to the questions: Who? To whom? From where? When?" (page 12). But we are not left with nothing. For, as Filson also points out, the author of Hebrews

> is to us what he has written. And that is a great deal to know and to have. It can spur modern Christians to renewed and increased awareness of what their faith can mean to them and what their faithfulness can mean to others (page 84).

Structure

Numerous outlines of the epistle have been set forward. One fascinating suggestion is made by Kistemaker who regards the epistle as a kind of sermon. He sees a four-point outline in the text itself at 2:17, and he suggests that the author develops each point on the basis of a quotation from the Psalms. His four points and their "texts" are:

1. Christ's humanity and unity with His brethren (Psalm 8:4-6; quoted in 2:6-8).

2. Christ's faith and faithfulness (Psalm 95:7-11; quoted in 3:7-11).

3. Christ's priesthood (Psalm 110:4; quoted first for discussion at 5:6).

4. Christ's offering of Himself (Psalm 40:6-8; quoted in 10:5-7).

Whether or not one should follow Kistemaker all the way, it is apparent that the Epistle to the Hebrews is thoroughly grounded in the Old Testament Scriptures in general and in the Psalms in particular.

Acknowledgements

A special acknowledgement of debt is due Dr. F. F. Bruce, the late Dr. Franz Delitzsch and the late Professor Robert Milligan, from whose commentaries I have drawn heavily and on which I have leaned with great profit. (All quotations from Bruce in the comments which follow are from his commentary unless otherwise stated.) Other commentaries and books have been used to advantage, but these have been my favorites. Delitzsch represents conservative scholarship of the past century; Bruce is unsurpassed in that role today. Milligan was of my own Restoration Movement background and, in my opinion, is not given the esteem as a scholar today which he certainly is due.

A note of thanks is also due Professor Homer Hailey, whose college lectures on the Scriptures led me in due course through the Epistle to the Hebrews, and whose biblical insight I will always remember with appreciation and respect. I should also like to thank Drs. Paul Southern, J. W. Roberts and Thomas H. Olbricht, who gave me valuable experience in the exegetical method of study.

To these all and many others my sincere appreciation for insights into this marvelous epistle. Any mistakes and misunderstandings in this commentary are my own. They only are original.

EDWARD FUDGE

HEBREWS

CHAPTER 1

1 God, who at sundry times and in divers manners spake in time past unto the fathers by the prophets,

---

EXPOSITION OF THE TEXT

CHAPTER ONE

In chapter one our author seems to have two points in mind. First, by showing Christ's superior position to angels, he sets forth also the superiority of the new covenant which Christ mediates and certifies over the old covenant which was mediated by angels. Second, he prepares the way for chapter two, in which he explains how and why the Son became lower than the angels for a brief period of time. A third consideration not specified by the writer of Hebrews but in accord with his epistle and perhaps also in his mind is that any revelation which claims angelic origin or authority must be measured in terms of that revelation which God has given through the Son — the Son who is better and higher than all angels.

1:1. The basic sentence in this verse and the next is "God hath spoken." **At sundry times** is from a single adverb in the original which meant "in many portions." Because God revealed His will in segments, revelation came from time to time as needed. It was the nature of the prophet that he spoke what God gave him to speak, and that was always "in part." **In divers manners** is also from a single adverb meaning "in many varied ways."

The adverbs modify the verb. God **spoke** (by prophets) to the fathers in many portions and in various ways. Amos

2 Hath in these last days spoken unto us by his Son,

---

gave God's message by oracles and direct statements from
God; Hosea by "typical" experiences in his own life; Habakkuk by arguments and discussion. Malachi spoke God's
word by questions and answers; Ezekiel by strange and
symbolic acts; Haggai by sermons and Zechariah by mystical
signs.

God addressed His people in parables and in illustra-
tions; by warnings and exhortations; by encouragements and
promises. By every possible method He spoke through the
prophets to the fathers. Yet the word was always fragmen-
tary and usually soon forgotten. When the Old Testament
closed, revelation was still incomplete. God was to speak
again, more fully and more effectively than He ever had
spoken in the prophets.

In time past is literally "of old," and refers to previous
ages of the world. The fathers were the Jewish forefathers
of the Hebrew Christians. The prophets included both the
writing prophets (such as those whose work Scripture pre-
serves) and the non-writing prophets (such as Nathan, Elijah, Elisha and others). The prophets were "mouths" for
God (Exodus 4:16; 7:1). They spoke His word, though at
times even they did not understand it (I Peter 1:10-12; see
Daniel 7:28; 12:8-10).

1:2. The phrase these last days refers to the Messianic
era, the age of fulfillment, and is literally "the last of these
days." The Jews divided time into the Present Age, of anticipation, and the Coming Age, of the Messiah. They expected the Messiah to come at the end of their Present Age.
When Christ came, however, the Coming Age crashed into
history and the Messianic era of fulfillment became a reality
(Hebrews 9:26-28). Peter's sermon on Pentecost formally
announced the beginning of these "last days" (Acts 2:14-36).

Here was one of the more puzzling elements of the
apostolic preaching for the Jews (and for people in general,
then and now). The Messianic era of fulfillment has now
begun with the resurrection of Christ and His ascension
into heaven, yet the temporal world continues even as it
decays. Men might expect the Present Age and the Coming

whom he hath appointed heir of all things, by whom also he made the worlds;

Age to meet at a given point, but certainly they do not expect them to overlap! Yet this is exactly what the New Testament declares, and it is this overlapping of Ages which creates the spiritual war for the Christian.

But while the "last days" have begun — one Man is already in heaven! — the consummation remains in the future and the old order continues to exist (II Peter 3:3-10). It is God's plan that the church use this interim to announce to the world that history has been given significance in Jesus of Nazareth, and that man can now ask God for reconciliation and have the assurance that He will give it through Christ. (On this age of the world in God's plan see also the introduction to chapters 9-11 in my **Helps on Romans.**)

God has **spoken unto us,** that is, to those living in this age, "to whom has come the very anticipated goal of the ages" (I Corinthians 10:11, my translation; see Mark 1:15; Luke 1:68-79; Luke 4:19/II Corinthians 6:2; Acts 3:24). **By His son** is literally "in a son" or "in one who is a son." Here is no mere prophet, but one who is Himself a Son and by nature the same as the Father.

Christ's very life and person expressed God (John 1:18). God has now revealed Himself fully, not partially. He has spoken grace and truth, a revelation superior to any given before (John 1:17). In Christ, God has spoken salvation, not only spoken it but accomplished it — in the unique life and sacrifice of the Son. The rest of chapter one exalts the Son of God, Jesus Christ our Lord, by showing His many-faceted ministry and position or "name."

God the Father has **appointed** or set or ordained Christ as **heir of all things. Heir** speaks of an inheritance and brings to mind the words of Psalm two, where the Son is given the nations for an inheritance. The same imagery occurs in Psalm 110, and our author will discuss that psalm several times, though usually with emphasis on Christ's priestly ministry.

By Christ God **made the worlds.** Christ is both originator and heir of all things. He is the Alpha and the Omega, the

3 Who being the brightness of his glory, and the express image of his person, and upholding all things by the word of his power, when he had by himself purged

---

author and finisher of creation as well as of faith. The **worlds** might mean the created universe (as in 11:3; see also John 1:3; Colossians 1:16-17) or literally "the ages" of time in which God's saving purpose is worked out. Both interpretations state what Scripture elsewhere affirms.

1:3. Christ is the **brightness of** the Father's **glory**. Literally "effulgence," this word means either that which radiates out from a light or the reflection which comes back. The former meaning is probably intended here. If we speak of God's glory, Christ is its very emenation and radiance. He is to the Father what rays are to a light, or flames to a fire, or beams to the sun. Without this Son, man is in the dark concerning God and salvation. God's magnificence as deity is fully seen in Jesus Christ who was God in human flesh (see John 14:9).

Christ is the **express image of** the Father's **person**. The word here translated **image** originally meant a stamp or seal, then the impression left by it. In the early centuries, the church engaged in great debates over the precise philosophical meanings of some of these terms. It is enough for us to know that Christ is an exact and complete representation of God because He is the Son, and that in that capacity He is perfectly sufficient to reveal God and to save man.

Christ is **upholding** all things; by Him all things consist or hold together (Colossians 1:17). **All things** may be translated "the universe." Christ's protectorate is all-inclusive. **The word of His power** is specifically a "spoken word," and the phrase might be translated "by His powerful spoken word." This is an active and powerful word which upholds the universe.

Christ accomplished man's redemption **by Himself**, through His own work of obedience. Our author elaborates on this statement in chapters eight through ten (see also Romans 5:12, 15-21). That Jesus **purged our sins** means that He "made a cleansing" or "accomplished a purification." The form of the verb indicates the words **by Himself**, and suggests a one-time action (see Hebrews 9:12-14, 26-28).

Because His work of redemption had been completed

our sins, sat down on the right hand of the Majesty on high;

4 Being made so much better than the angels, as he hath by inheritance obtained a more excellent name than they.

(2:9; 6:20; 7:26-27; 9:24-28; 10:12-14; 12:2), Christ **sat down.** Unlike the Levitical priests who stood daily in an imperfect and temporary service, Christ made atonement for all men and then took His seat forever (10:11-12). **The right hand** signifies authority; see notes on verse 13. **The Majesty** refers to God the Father. Our author follows a Jewish custom of referring to Jehovah by a euphemism, out of respect for the sacred name.

1:4. Christ has been **made so much better than the angels,** which it will be our writer's business to explain in the remainder of chapter one. This verse contains two Greek words which express comparison (see also 7:20-22; 8:6 and 10:25). Christ is as much better than angels as His name is more excellent than theirs. The author will show how much **more excellent name** Christ possesses **than they,** and to that same extent he will show Christ to be higher in rank than the angels themselves.

The writer has introduced his first point: Christ is a spokesman superior to prophets or angels — because He is the Son. He was active in creation. He is God's very substance and image. He has accomplished a perfect work of complete redemption, and He has now taken His inherited seat as universal heir and Lord at God's right hand in heaven. He is Prophet (verse two), Priest (verse three) and King (verse three).

Christ's name is far higher than those of the heavenly emissaries, but why would our author need to make this point? It has already been mentioned that many in the ancient world thought of angels as lords over the present world system. Others worshipped angels. Still others regarded Christ as simply one in an ascending order of angels. The former overrated angels by giving them what belongs to the Son; the latter underrated the Son by considering Him an angel (an error propagated today by the so-called Jehovah's Witness cult). The following verses put angels and the Son in proper perspective.

5 For unto which of the angels said he at any time,
Thou art my Son, this day have I begotten thee? And again,
I will be to him a Father, and he shall be to me a Son?

1:5a. To no angel did God ever say, **Thou are my son,
this day have I begotten thee**; but He said it to the Son in
Psalm 2:7. This Messianic psalm describes man's rejection of
Christ and God (verses 1-3; see Acts 4:25-28). It also fore-
tells God's triumph through His Christ ("Anointed," verses
4-9; see Revelation 12:5; 19:15). And it gives a double pronouncement in view of the Messianic judgment to come
(verses 10-12). The same psalm is quoted also at Acts 13:33
of the resurrection of Christ, and at Hebrews 5:5 of Christ's
divine installment as high priest. It seems to underlie the
heavenly voice at Christ's baptism (along with Isaiah 42:1)
and at His transfiguration (with Isaiah 42:1 and possibly
Deuteronomy 18:15ff).

Emphasis here is on **Son**, stressing Christ's nature and
position, and on the first person pronoun "I," emphasizing
the divine origin of His appointment. Christ is God's own
Son in essence by eternal nature. He was God in the flesh
through a miraculous conception. He is ranking Son and Man
in glory through His resurrection and a divine decree.

Of course the psalmist did not understand all of this,
and his words may have been partially appreciated through
a lesser fulfillment in his own day. But their full meaning
is seen only in the light of the resurrection and ascension
of Christ. The same Holy Spirit which guided the prophets
(II Peter 1:21) also led the apostles into the meaning of
their writings (I Peter 1:10-12), as well as the significance
of the gospel events involving Jesus the Christ (John 14:26;
15:26; 16:12-14; see also John 2:19-22; 12:12-16; 13:6-7; Luke
24:31-32, 44-45).

1:5b. **I will be to him a father, and he shall be to me a
son.** These words are quoted from II Samuel 7:14, an oracle
of Nathan concerning David's royal son. The promise referred partially to Solomon (I Kings 2:23-24; I Chronicles
28:5-7) but, as many other Old Testament statements, found
perfect fulfillment only in Christ. Both "I" and "He" are
emphatic, stressing the personal relationship between the
speaker and the one of whom He speaks. **To him** and **to me**

6 And again, when he bringeth in the first begotten into the world, he saith, And let all the angels of God worship him.

7 And of the angels he saith, Who maketh his angels spirits, and his ministers a flame of fire.

8 But unto the Son he saith, Thy throne, O God, is for ever and ever: a sceptre of righteousness is the sceptre of thy kingdom.

9 Thou hast loved righteousness, and hated iniquity;

---

reflect Hebrew style; the statement means simply "I shall be his father; he shall be my son." The Son of God was the prophetic son of David (Matthew's gospel emphasizes this: see 1:1, 20; 9:27; 12:23; 15:22; 20:30-31; 21:9; 21:15; also 12:3; 22:41ff). The statements quoted in verse five describe a Son, not mere angels.

1:6. Again could be placed at the beginning this verse, as in the King James and Revised Standard versions, introducing another Old Testament citation; or with the verb, as in the American Standard and New American Standard versions. The phrase has been regarded as referring to the incarnation, the resurrection and the second advent. Angels are associated with all three events in Scripture. The point is that they worship Him. All the angels of God, of every rank and order, are commanded to worship him, a fact which points to His superiority over them. The quotation might be from a Greek version of Deuteronomy 32:43 or of Psalm 97:7. No doubt the first readers of the epistle recognized it.

1:7. In this verse and the next, two words are used which together mean "on the one hand" and "on the other hand." A contrast is intended here between angels, who are ministers or servants, and the Son who is so much more. The quotation is from Psalm 104:4.

1:8. Psalm 45:6-7 is applied to Christ, identifying Him as eternal God whose throne is for ever and ever, and as righteous King. His kingdom is one of righteousness (Hebrews 7:2-3; Isaiah 9:7; 11:4-5).

1:9. In the flesh, Christ loved righteousness and hated iniquity (see 10:5-10; Isaiah 53:11-12). Because of His per-

therefore God, even thy God, hath anointed thee with the oil of gladness above thy fellows.

10 And, Thou, Lord, in the beginning hast laid the foundation of the earth; and the heavens are the works of thine hands:

11 They shall perish; but thou remainest; and they all shall wax old as doth a garment;

12 And as a vesture shalt thou fold them up, and they shall be changed: but thou are the same, and thy years shall not fail.

---

fect obedience, Jesus was anointed ("Christ-ed") by God and exalted above every creature (see Philippians 2:8-11). The oil of gladness probably represents an occasion of festivity as well as that of coronation. Psalm 45 seems to have originally celebrated the marriage of the king, though again its deepest meaning is understood only in the light of the Son. Along this line, compare Hebrews 12:22-24 (see notes on "general assembly") with Revelation 19:1-10. The chief point of the verse ought not to be overlooked in the midst of details.

1:10-12. These three verses are quoted from Psalm 102:25-27. In the passage the psalmist calls on Jehovah to come to his rescue, and appeals to God's eternal nature in pleading for the deliverance of his own life. This is only one of many passages addressed to or regarding Jehovah in the Old Testament which are applied to Christ in the New Testament.

Because Christ is creator, He is also eternal — though all His creation will change with age and finally pass away. He laid the foundation of the earth and His hands arranged the heavens, but when these things perish (see 12:26-28) His years will not fail (7:24-25). When they are all changed He will remain the same (13:8).

Again the contrast is between the Son and the angels (verse seven), who have no such traits or legitimate claims. They are rather part of that creation which He has made and have life only through His will.

13 But to which of the angels said he at any time, Sit on my right hand, until I make thine enemies thy footstool?

14 Are they not all ministering spirits, sent forth to minister for them who shall be heirs of salvation?

1:13. This is a quotation of Psalm 110:1, the Old Testament passage most quoted or referred to in the New Testament Scriptures. It is quoted in Acts 2:34-35; Mark 12:36; Hebrews 1:13, and seems to be in mind in Mark 14:62; Acts 7:55; Romans 8:34; Ephesians 1:20; Colossians 3:1; Hebrews 1:3; 8:1; 10:12; 12:2 and I Peter 3:22. As noted already at verse five, many psalms which had partial fulfillment or significance in their original historical settings are fully understood in the New Testament writings through the life, death, resurrection and coronation of Christ.

The figure of the **right hand** is common in the Psalms, sometimes referring to a place of honor as here (see Psalm 16:11; 45:9; 80:17). Most of the time the term refers to strength or security from God given to the one of whom it is used. The resurrected Jesus, now made Christ, was given a position equaled only by that of God Himself (I Corinthians 15:27). He is God's Right-Hand Man.

In the Old Testament we see the custom of the conquered king prostrating himself to kiss the conqueror's feet (Psalm 2:12), or the victor putting his feet on his captive's neck (Joshua 10:24) so that the captive is made his **footstool.** One day every knee will bow before Christ and every tongue will confess His lordship (Philippians 2:10-11; I Corinthians 15:24-25). The angels will be in that number; the Son is made so much better than them all (verse four).

1:14. This question is worded in the Greek to indicate that the author expects an affirmative answer. Angels **all,** regardless of rank, are **ministering spirits.** But Christ is so much more. They are **sent forth** by a higher authority, perhaps even by the Son at God's right hand. Their work is to serve, **to minister for** Christians, **who shall be heirs of salvation.** Our writer says literally that they are "sent for service on behalf of those who are about to receive salvation as an inheritance." If angels serve the saints, how much more do they serve the Son! And how greatly superior is His position and name to theirs.

Christ is Prophet of prophets — God has spoken in Him for these last days. He is Priest of priests — by Himself He made atonement for sins. He is King of kings — seated at God's right hand, reigning over a kingdom of righteousness. Old Testament Scripture shows Him to be God's divine Son, David's prophetic descendant, and worthy of worship. Whereas angels are messengers, Christ is eternally Lord and divine King. As everlasting Creator of all things, He is also now victorious Vicegerent at God's right hand. The voice from heaven at Christ's transfiguration aptly sums up our author's argument in this first chapter: "Hear ye Him!"

CHAPTER TWO

Having demonstrated in chapter one the superiority of Christ the Son over the serving angels, our writer concludes in 2:1-4 (which would have been placed more appropriately as the ending of the first chapter) with an exhortation and a warning.

His arguments is of a type commonly employed by the Jewish teachers of the time, and was called by them an argument **qal wahomer** — "from the light to the weighty." A statement is made concerning a "lighter" matter, which then is inferred to be even more certainly true of a matter of greater or "heavier" importance.

Jesus' statements concerning the Father's benevolence follow this kind of reasoning (Matthew 6:25-31; 7:9-11), as do His remarks about working on the Sabbath (Matthew 12:10-12). Paul uses the same type of reasoning to show the security of the true believer (Romans 5:8-10) and the abundant provisions of divine grace (Romans 5:15-21). The author of Hebrews later reasons the same way regarding Christ's unique priesthood (chapter seven) and all-sufficient sacrifice for sin (9:13-14), Christian discipline (12: 9-10), and the reverence which should accompany those who are heirs of the unshakeable kingdom (12:25-29).

In these verses he speaks of two agents by whom God's word has come, and of the consequences of failing to heed that word — especially as spoken by the Son. If Christ's position is far greater than that given the angels (as has

CHAPTER 2

1 Therefore we ought to give the more earnest heed to the things which we have heard, lest at any time we should let them slip.

2 For if the word spoken by angels was steadfast,

---

been shown in chapter one), punishment for ignoring or rejecting His message must be far greater than that given for irreverence of the angelic word.

2:1. **Therefore** is literally "on account of this"; that is, because of the greatness of the Son and in view of the point to follow. **Ought** is not the simple word for an obligation but the stronger word which means "it is imperative" or "it is necessary." **To give the more earnest heed** translates a verb meaning "to pay careful attention" and an adverb (based on an adjective in the comparative degree) meaning "even more extremely." The result is an exceptionally strong exhortation. "Because of these things," he is saying, "it is absolutely necessary for us to be extremely careful to pay attention."

His readers are to hold to **the things which** they **have heard** from the Son by means of His apostles. **Lest we let them slip** is better translated "lest we drift away (from them)," as in the later versions. The word translated **slip** was used by Greek writers of an arrow slipping out of the quiver, of snow sliding, of foul language slipping into a conversation or, in medical contexts, of food slipping down the windpipe instead of the esophagus. The writer urges extreme care lest his readers **slip** from steadfast obedience and trust in the Son.

Their danger, and that of many other New Testament readers then and now, was that of slipping from trust in the Son's finished work of salvation by His own perfect-life obedience and sacrifice to a reliance on their own performance based on a meritorious view of salvation. The same caution applies equally well to slipping from active obedience to careless disobedience or disregard.

2:2. **For** indicates the basis of the warning. **The word spoken by angels** would include every divine message de-

**and every transgression and disobedience received a just
recompence of reward;**

**3 How shall we escape, if we neglect so great salvation;
which at the first began to be spoken by the Lord, and was**

---

livered by angels, but has special reference to the Law of
Moses which was delivered by means of angels and was
highly esteemed by the Jews for that reason (Psalm 68:17;
Deuteronomy 33:2; Acts 7:53; Galatians 3:19). **Steadfast** here
means reliable, dependable or strong. God's word by angels was always a sure word which came to pass.

Transgression refers to a violation of an express command and **disobedience** refers to a refusal or neglect to
obey. The former stresses the act of disobedience; the latter
stresses the careless or rebellious attitude which prompts it.
Punishment was certain in either case under the Law.

God's punishment of sin was always the **just** or fair
reward of sin. It was never arbitrary, but always in keeping
with divine justice and holiness. **Recompense** indicates a
payment of wages earned. The wages of sin is death — that
is the fair payment earned by sin. The man who gets "what
he has coming to him" will never be saved.

2:3. **We** are those to whom the Son has spoken in these
last days, and the pronoun is here emphasized. To **neglect**
salvation is to fail to show concern and care for it. Neglect
is a positive wrong consisting of a lack of action. By doing
nothing one does wrong. The tense of the verb here views
life as a whole — this is more an attitude governing all of
life than it is a single or specific act (see 6:7-12; 10:28-29).
Generalities, of course, are always manifested in specifics.
A single act of neglect suggests an attitude of the same
and should be cause for repentance and diligence.

We have a **salvation** which is **so great** for a number
of reasons. It comes from a great spokesman (chapter one).
It involves a great work of redemption (1:3; 2:9, 14). This
great work brought great results (2:10, 15, 17). So great a
salvation carries a judgment equally great for those who re-
ject it (see 6:4-8; 10:28-31; also Mark 16:16; Romans 1:17-18;
II Corinthians 2:15-16). This salvation **was spoken first by
the Lord** Jesus Christ Himself. It was repeated and **con-**

confirmed unto us by them that heard him;

4 God also bearing them witness, both with signs and wonders, and with divers miracles, and gifts of the Holy Ghost, according to his own will?

5 For unto the angels hath he not put in subjection

---

firmed to the recipients of this epistle by chosen apostles who had heard him speak. The verb translated "confirm" is a form of the same word "steadfast" in verse two. Christ's word is a sure word.

2:4. Freely translated, our author says that God added witness upon witness, piling testimony together. He did this by signs (stressing the spiritual meaning of the acts) and wonders (stressing the effect on those who saw), various kinds of miracles (stressing the might involved in accomplishing these signs and wonders; literally the word is "powers"), and spiritual gifts of the Holy Spirit which were given to the early church (see I Corinthians 12; Romans 12).

All this was according to God's own will. He confirmed the supernatural message of a resurrected and ascended Savior by supernatural demonstrations of power — because He willed to do so. The absence of such signs today speaks not of God's power but of His will. He could if He would. But apparently He will not because He "wills" not. For a discussion of the Biblical teaching on this point see my booklet Speaking in Tongues.

The answer to the original question must be that there is no escape. If the lesser word of angels was sure and violations of it were strictly punished, there is absolutely no escape for one who carelessly regards the great salvation spoken by the superior Son. Let each true believer hold fast to the Son of God in constant diligence, trusting His work of salvation for total deliverance from sin and yielding to His voice in all things.

2:5. At the beginning of the remarks on chapter one the comment was made that those verses prepared the way for chapter two, in which the author would tell how the Son became lower than angels for a brief period of time, and explain why. By the end of the first chapter the original Jewish readers might very well have asked, "If the Son

the world to come, whereof we speak.

6 But one in a certain place testified, saying, What is
man, that thou art mindful of him? or the son of man, that
thou visitest him?

7 Thou madest him a little lower than the angels;
thou crownedst him with glory and honor, and didst set
him over the works of thy hands:

8 Thou hast put all things in subjection under his

---

is so much greater than the angels, why did He become a
man and die?"

Beginning with verse five the author answers this
question. In the process he shows the intended creation
glory and dignity of man, a position never realized fully
after the Fall by any man except Jesus Christ. He demonstrates how Jesus now occupies this place of prominence,
and how, by virtue of His accomplishments, all men may
enjoy their intended state of glory.

There are Biblical indications that the angels have a
hand in God's administration of the present world-order
(Daniel 10:20-21; 12:1; Ephesians 6:12). We know that
various Jewish sects before and after Christ assigned such
a role to angels, and the epistle to the Colossians indicates
that certain gentile teachers did the same. Be that as it may,
God did not plan the glorified world to come for the benefit
of the angels, but for man. The intended glory of man is expressed in terms of all things being put in subjection to him
(see Romans 8:19-25; II Peter 3:7, 10, 13-14; Revelation
21:1ff).

2.6. David is quoted from Psalm 8:5-7 to establish this
point. God is interested in and mindful of man. He visits
him in blessing and judgment. The son of man in this psalm
is simply a poetic expression for man.

2:7. Man was made but a little lower than the angels.
He was crowned by the Creator with glory and honor. He
was set over the works of God's hands (see Genesis 1:26-28).
This was man's intended exalted position as first created
by God for paradise glory.

2:8. God put all things in subjection under man's feet,

feet. For in that he put all in subjection under him, he left
nothing that is not put under him. But now we see not
yet all things put under him.

9 But we see Jesus, who was made a little lower
than the angels for the suffering of death, crowned with

---

according to the psalmist. Our writer reasons as follows. If
God really put all things in subjection under him, nothing
is excluded from man's dominion and oversight. Yet if we
look about us we do not see all things under man's control—
yet. Man is not master of his environment and world,
though he is frequently its corrupter and polluter. Man
does not enjoy paradise glory and dominion. To say this
is to state the obvious. But does this mean that God's purpose
has been thwarted? Is there anywhere a man who is over
all things — in complete control?

2:9. We do not see ourselves in that position — at
least not at the present time. But we do see Jesus, and He
is crowned with glory and honor! Is the mighty Son of
chapter one — that Son so much better than the angels — a
man? Yes! For He was made a little lower than the angels,
even to the suffering of death, that by the grace of God He
could die for every man — then give all who would follow
Him their intended glory and dominion.

Jesus became a representative man. In Him, God found
a man who gave what He had always wanted from man
but which no man had ever given — a human life fully
and always dedicated to pleasing God. In Christ, man's glorified potential was fully realized. This glory was not even
planned for angels. It was not intended for other heavenly
beings, earthly creatures or occupants of the subterranean
depths. It was the Creator's original intention for man. And
now one man is in that position. One man has a foothold in
glory! And because He is a representative man, acting on
behalf of all mankind, His people will one day enjoy the
same position of glory.

The expression a little lower than the angels is used
in two senses in this passage. When it is said that man was
put a little lower than the angels, the expression indicated
his exalted position — it is but a little lower than the angels
(and the original psalm had the general word for "God"

glory and honor; that he by the grace of God should taste death for every man.

10 For it became him, for whom are all things, and by whom are all things, in bringing many sons unto glory, to make the captain of their salvation perfect through suffering.

11 For both he that sanctifieth and they who are sanctified are all of one: for which cause he is not ashamed to call them brethren,

---

instead of "angels"). But when it is said of Jesus that He became a little lower than the angels, the direction is reversed. For Jesus is the Son, far greater than the angels. To say that He became lower than angels is to say that He was humiliated, that He emptied Himself, that He condescended (Philippians 2:5ff). It is also to say that He became a man— like ourselves and for our benefit.

2:10. It was becoming, fitting and proper for **him for whom are all things and by whom are all things** (Revelation 4:11; Romans 11:36; I Corinthians 8:6; II Corinthians 5:18) to bring **many sons to glory** by making Jesus their **perfect** forerunner or **captain,** even **through suffering.**

In becoming a representative man, Jesus willingly became of the same stuff as mankind in general. He became a brother to man, of the seed of David according to the flesh. In becoming a man, Jesus also took on suffering and death, both inevitable characteristics of mankind. Yet because of His sinless life, His death was able to count as our death. And by suffering death, Christ was able to bring many sons to glory — going ahead of them Himself as Captain, experiencing first the suffering of death but then the glory of resurrection and installment at God's right hand — the same kind of glory they, too, will one day enjoy because of Him.

2:11. **He that sanctifieth** is Christ and **they who are sanctified** are saints or Christians. Both they and Christ are **all of one** Father — God. For this reason Christ **is not ashamed** or embarrassed **to call them brethren.** Christ did not call us His brethren because He approved of our lives or agreed with all our ideas. Brotherhood is not dependent

12 Saying, I will declare thy name unto my brethren, in the midst of the church will I sing praise unto thee.

13 And again, I will put my trust in him. And again, Behold I and the children which God hath given me.

---

on such things, though endorsement involves them. Christ did not endorse the thoughts and behavior of all his brethren; He simply called them brothers. The basis of brotherhood is a common fatherhood. Those who have the same father should not be embarrassed to call one another brethren.

2:12. The words of Psalm 22:22 are quoted in the mouth of Jesus. The psalmist calls on God for deliverance from enemies. He hopefully affirms that he will yet **declare** God's **name** among his **brethren** in the congregation of God's people. The word usually translated **church** refers numerous times in the Greek Old Testament to the Jews in solemn assembly.

Psalm 22 is quite descriptive of Jesus, and the entire psalm was generally understood by Christ and His apostles as predictive of the suffering of the Messiah and the glory which would follow. Jesus suffered personally, was delivered by God, and now lives to declare God's salvation among His brethren.

2:13. Words similar to **I will put my trust in him** are found in the Greek Old Testament at II Samuel 22:3; Psalm 18:2 and Isaiah 8:17. The point of the quotation here is that Jesus, like His human brothers, had to depend on God and trust in Him (see Mark 14:32-36). Luke only of the Evangelists records the dying words of Christ: "Father, into thy hands I commend my spirit" (23:46) — and Luke's Gospel highlights the humanity of Jesus and His identification with mankind throughout. The particular verb form given in Jesus' statement in the verse just mentioned stresses the extreme personal trust Jesus felt in committing His life to the Father's care (see also I Peter 2:23; 4:19).

The next quotation is certainly from Isaiah 8:18 (which argues for Isaiah 8:17 in the previous citation). The meaning here is that Jesus is one with His human brethren in obedience to God as Father. The words of this quotation

14 Forasmuch then as the children are partakers of flesh and blood, he also himself likewise took part of the same; that through death he might destroy him that had the power of death, that is, the devil;

15 And deliver them who through fear of death were all their lifetime subject to bondage.

16 For verily he took not on him the nature of angels;

---

should not be pressed too far. Jesus is brother to the saints, not their father.

2:14. Since God's other **children are** necessarily **partakers of flesh and blood,** with all that is implied in that statement, Christ **also took part of the same.** He died, as they do, but **through** His **death he destroyed** or nullified the strength of the **devil** who **had the power of death** over man because of sin. Since Jesus had no sin of His own, the devil had no power over Him. When Christ entered the grave, therefore, He was not bound. Rather He walked in free-handed, picked up the keys and came out again in triumph! (See Revelation 1:17-18.)

2:15. Because Jesus rose from the dead, death can no longer hold its former terror for the man who trusts in Jesus. By His resurrection, Christ was able to **deliver** mankind from the **bondage** in which he is bound **all his lifetime;** that is, the bondage of the **fear of death.** Because one man has conquered death, Satan is immobilized and all men are potentially free of death's rule.

The same power which brought Jesus out of Hades will also bring out His saints (see Romans 8:11; II Corinthians 4:14; I Thessalonians 4:14). It is interesting that the ancient Greeks called their burial-ground a "necropolis" — city of the dead, but that since Christ we call it a "cemetery" — sleeping place. One man has been to the city of the dead and returned! Because He did, we will.

2:16. The word translated **took on** may mean either "to take hold of for oneself" — the idea represented in the King James Version, or "to take hold of someone to help him" — as probably is the case here. From this second meaning the word may mean simply "to have an interest in, show concern for, or help" someone. It is true that Jesus

but he took on him the seed of Abraham.

**17 Wherefore in all things it behoved him to be made
like unto his brethren, that he might be a merciful and
faithful high priest in things pertaining to God, to make**

---

took on Himself the nature of man and not angel, and
verses 5-15 have been given to that theme. This verse seems
to speak, however, of Jesus taking hold of man to help him.
Angels did not need redemption and apparently fallen
angels can not be redeemed — but man both needed it and
would receive it. Jesus became a man to accomplish man's
needed redemption (1:3; 2:9; notes on 10:1-14).

Jesus was born to save His Jewish people from their
sins (Matthew 1:21) and to fulfill the promises made to the
fathers (Acts 13:32-33; Romans 15:8). To that end He
became one of **the seed of Abraham.** But by the grace of
God He also tasted death for every man (Hebrews 2:9),
so that gentiles as well as Jews may praise God for His
mercy (Romans 15:9).

2:17. **Wherefore,** because Jesus took on the responsibility of saving man, **in all things** it was necessary for Him to
be made like unto his brethren. God's design for man's
salvation consisted of sending a representative man who
could do for man what man had been unable to do for
himself — live an acceptable life before God. Because
Jesus was this chosen and well-beloved Servant of the
Father, and in order to carry out this divine mission, He
became in every respect like His human brethren, though
without sin.

He was divine, God in the flesh, and we must never
forget that. But we should not forget either that He was
fully human. Jesus was a man, with every human temptation,
desire and sorrow. If His deity had precluded any of these
He could not have been a truly representative man and
could have become neither Savior not even a fair example.

Because He did fully identify with His human brethren,
yet remained faithful to God in all His life, He became a
perfect **high priest,** both **merciful** to man and **faithful** or
reliable in His relationship to God. As high priest He first

reconciliation for the sins of the people.

18   For in that he himself hath suffered being tempted, he is able to succor them that are tempted.

---

made reconciliation for the sins of all His people, then became Mediator on their behalf before God.

2:18. Because he himself hath suffered, being tempted through every possible allurement and enticement of Satan including an undeserved death, he has the power and is able to succor or render aid and comfort to His people when they are tempted. He became a son of man that we might become sons of God. He took our place, died our death — that we might enjoy His life and the blessings it made possible.

But He not only died for us — He first lived for us. While this point is frequently overlooked, it is this which made the first possible and meaningful. It is only by His perfect life — lived on our behalf and in our stead, then offered to the Father and accepted by Him — that we can be made accepted, for our own imperfect lives are never perfectly acceptable to the Father. Salvation is by the grace of God from beginning to end, and it was by the grace of God that Jesus tasted death for every man.

Moses could give a law but only Jesus could live that law. Unless we see Him in this light He will mean little more to us than Moses did to the Jew. And great as Moses was, he was not in the same category with the Son who became man. This point our author develops in the next chapter.

CHAPTER THREE

The writer has shown Jesus to be superior to the prophets as a spokesman for God. As the Son, Christ's name or position is far greater than that of any angel. Yet He became one of us, to bring us to our intended glory. Through His own suffering and temptations He was qualified to serve perfectly as priest and comforter to His suffering and tempted brethren on earth.

Now the author turns to other matters (led, of course,

CHAPTER 3

1 Wherefore, holy brethren, partakers of the heavenly

---

by the Spirit of God). Moses was the chief character of the Old Covenant, and was respected by the Hebrews as the foremost leader of their religion and life. Jesus is prophet and priest of the New Covenant, and Christians are to be faithful to Him in all things. The Hebrew Christians were being tempted to leave Christ and return to Moses. To prevent this, chapter three shows Christ's superiority over Moses. It shows the possibility of apostasy and destruction, based on the former example of God's Old Testament people under Moses. The chapter then urges extreme caution in maintaining a faithful heart lest the Christian, too, fall by disbelief.

3:1. **Wherefore,** or because of what has gone before — specifically because of the divine appointment of Christ as perfect prophet and because of His absolute perfection as sympathetic and faithful priest — the admonition follows. The **holy brethren** are Christians. The phrase literally means "brothers who are set apart (from the world and sin) and are dedicated (to the service of God through Christ)." Christians are saints or holy ones, not because of their own achievements in attaining purity of life (see I Corinthians 1:2; 6:11), though that is a necessity, but because God has called them holy, in Jesus Christ. Christ is made unto us "sanctification" or holiness (I Corinthians 1:30). We are holy in Him.

Yet we are commanded to become holy, just as God is holy (I Peter 1:15-16). We are to perfect holiness in the fear of God (II Corinthians 7:1). Without holiness no man can see God (Hebrews 12:14). In the economy of the New Testament, however, God first pronounces men to be what He desires (on the basis of the finished work of Christ and their union with Him) and then causes them to become what He has already called them.

The term "saints" is one of the most frequently used descriptions of God's people in the New Testament. The word is always in the plural; one does not read of "Saint So-and-so." All God's people are saints, as described above. It is

calling, consider the Apostle and High Priest of our profession, Christ Jesus.

---

possible that the tendency of modern Christians to neglect this term in their common vocabulary has contributed to the lack of sanctification in the church today. We will do no harm, and perhaps a great deal of good, to revive the usage of Scriptural terms and phrases.

The saints are **partakers** or partners in **the heavenly calling.** Their heavenly invitation to be God's people leads them, in response to the gospel, to become partners and sharers in a heavenly way of life. Now the writer urges them to **consider Christ Jesus.** The word translated **consider** means to look at something or someone with great care. It involves not only looking at, but thinking about. One must spend time to fulfill this word. The object of such contemplation is here Christ Jesus.

Many times in Scripture the writer makes a point of emphasis by the order of words. Frequently the term **Christ Jesus** points to Jesus, not in His earthly ministry, but as the Christ at God's right hand — the resurrected and glorified Jesus of Nazareth. On the other hand, the expression **Jesus Christ** sometimes (but not always) stresses the work, or ministry, or person of Jesus as a man and as one of us. Here we are to consider our heavenly Lord: in all His offices, His splendor, His rank and His glory.

We are specifically to consider Christ as **the Apostle and High Priest of our profession.** The term **apostle** means one sent or a messenger. Jesus was sent by the Father to be Savior of the world (I John 4:14 and other passages). Moses also was sent by God to accomplish a typical "salvation" of God's people from bondage (Exodus 3:10), though Moses is never called an **apostle.**

Jesus is also our **High Priest,** and the writer has spoken briefly of this office in the previous chapter. Later he will develop the thought in detail. Here he entreats us to reflect on Christ Jesus: as Apostle — sent by God's authority to man; as High Priest — going before God on man's behalf; in all things — superior to every previous agent of God.

Our profession or confession is first our oral acknowl-

2 Who was faithful to him that appointed him, as also
Moses was faithful in all his house.

3 For this man was counted worthy of more glory
than Moses, inasmuch as he who hath builded the house hath
more honor than the house.

4 For every house is builded by some man; but he
that built all things is God.

5 And Moses verily was faithful in all his house, as a

---

edgement of faith in Jesus as Christ and Lord (see Matthew
16:16; Romans 10:9-10; II Corinthians 9:13; I Timothy 6:
12-13; Hebrews 4:14; 10:23). Then it is our state of life
based on that confession, a profession or declaration of the
faith which has been confessed.

3:2. Christ **was faithful** or reliable or trustworthy with
reference to God the Father, who **appointed him** apostle and
priest. **Moses also was faithful** to God **in all his house.** The
writer does not minimize the faithfulness or the function of
Moses. He praises and commends Moses for faithful service.
But he then shows, on the basis of the heavenly realities,
that Christ is far superior to Moses by virtue of His greater
person and function.

3:3. Christ is **counted worthy of more glory than Moses,**
not because Moses was unfaithful, for he was not, but because of the inherent function of both men in God's plan.
The man who builds a house **hath more honor than the house.**
We admire a beautiful building, but we regard more highly
the architect who designed it and the superintendent who
saw it rise.

3:4. So far as the work of salvation is concerned, the
one who builds **all things is God.** He is the grand architect
and superintendent of the entire scheme of redemption. He
is its originator and its goal. The Word which became flesh
was one with God the Father. Therefore Christ, who was
that Word, is the builder of the house, while Moses — though
faithful — was a part in the divine house.

3:5. Christ is superior to Moses in other points as well.
Moses verily was faithful, but in God's household, **as a**
servant and as a member of the household. His faithfulness

servant, for a testimony of those things which were to be
spoken after;

6 But Christ as a son over his own house; whose house
are we, if we hold fast the confidence and the rejoicing
of the hope firm unto the end.

---

to God served as a testimony to the reliability and trust-
worthiness of the message which he spoke from God. The
point here is based on Numbers 12:6-8, which is quoted
in part. There God testified to the faithfulness of Moses and
rewarded that faithfulness by speaking directly with Moses
in revealing His will. Moses' personal faithfulness as a work-
er in God's house served as a witness to the word which he
revealed from God.

But Christ is a son (not a servant) over (not in and
part of) his own house (not that of someone else). Now we
learn what is meant by the house so far as Christ is concerned. We, the church, God's people under Christ are the
house of God (I Timothy 3:15). Christ promised to "build" it
(Matthew 16:18), and He began that work on Pentecost. The
church is composed of "living stones" (I Peter 2:5; Ephesians
2:20) — those individuals who by faith and baptism have
come into union with Christ, have become members of His
spiritual body and, collectively, are His church. Moses was
a faithful servant in the Old Testament "house" of God (and
of Christ), but Christ is the faithful Son over His own
house. He is far superior to Moses, though Moses was a great
and faithful man of God.

But there is a divine if, so far as we are concerned.
We are His house, if we hold fast the confidence, the boldness based on inner assurance, and the rejoicing or boasting
of the hope firm unto the end. This is the message of the entire Bible and is particularly the theme of the book of
Hebrews. The reward is of grace, but it depends on faith.
And a saving faith is one which trusts and obeys until the
very end. It is not enough to begin, only to fall along the
way. Saving faith, true grounds of rejoicing, a genuine
hope — all these depend on steadfastness and continued
trust throughout life. The Hebrew Christians urgently needed that lesson. We are no less in need of it today.

7   Wherefore (as the Holy Ghost saith, To day if ye
will hear his voice,

8   Harden not your hearts, as in the provocation, in the
day of temptation in the wilderness:

3:7-8. As an incentive to steadfastness, our author points
to the example of God's people under Moses (see also I
Corinthians 10:1-13). If they fell from God's favor through
disbelief, the same fate could befall God's people today.
Wherefore (as the Holy Ghost saith in Psalm 95:7-11), To
day if ye will hear his voice, harden not your hearts.

Psalm 95 is a call to worship God. The psalmist bases
his call on God's deity (verse three), His might as creator
and sustainer (verses four through six) and His election of
and covenant relationship with Israel (verse seven). He
then warns against a hard or disobedient heart, which he
says will lead only to destruction. This happened to the
fathers in the wilderness, the psalmist points out, and it
can happen to God's people in his day. Now the psalmist's
point is made (using his own words) by the writer to the
Hebrews, who applies it to the believers of his day. God's
people have fallen before through unbelief and an evil
heart. They can do the same again.

Today those who hear his voice are not to harden their
hearts. This happened with the Jews in the provocation
(Hebrew: Massah) in the day of temptation (Hebrew: Meri-
bah) in the wilderness. The event mentioned here is recorded in Exodus 17:1-7. The unbelief of the Jews then was essentially a lack of trust. They doubted that God, who had
called them from Egypt, would provide for them in the
wilderness and see them safely to the promised land. This
lack of faith led to murmuring. That murmuring was a provocation of God and was sin. Christians are exhorted not to
distrust God, murmur and sin, but to have full confidence
in Him. In that confident trust they are to do His will as
fully and exactly as possible.

The Hebrew Christians were in danger of leaving Christ
for Moses. The analogy here suggests that back of their
threatened apostasy was a basic lack of trust in the work
of Christ as perfect sacrifice, priest and Savior. They were

9 When your fathers tempted me, proved me, and saw
my works forty years.

10 Wherefore I was grieved with that generation, and
said, They do alway err in their heart; and they have not
known my ways.

11 So I sware in my wrath, They shall not enter into
my rest.)

12 Take heed, brethren, lest there be in any of you an
evil heart of unbelief, in departing from the living God.

---

not confident of their standing before God. Because their
basis of salvation was the finished redemptive work of the
Son, such lack of confidence reflected a fundamental lack
of faith in Christ. This unbelief was sinful — and it was the
same kind of sin which led to the Jews' destruction centuries
before in the wilderness.

3:9-11. Our author is still quoting from Psalm 95. The
fathers in the wilderness tempted God, proved Him in the
evil sense of putting Him to the test and saw His works for
forty years so that they should have no excuse. They
grieved God by distrusting Him. Because of this unbelief
God swore in His wrath that they would not enter into His
rest. Chapter four will discuss the meaning of God's rest.
Here the reference is made without elaboration.

3:12. Rather than take heed, we would say (almost
literally) "look out!" An evil heart of unbelief is a heart, or
disposition, or spirit, which does not so trust God that it
accepts what He says with confidence and then walks with
trust in Him and in His word. Departing is from a word
closely related to that which gives "apostasy." The child
of God can become so corrupted by a distrustful and unfaithful heart that he finally forsakes God completely.

Such distrust of Christ can lead to apostasy in two direc-
tions. Some who begin to doubt their acceptance on the basis
of Christ's perfect life and blood will despair of all hope
and go back into sin and the world. Others will seek to help
or add to their spiritual stature by their own strict observance of rules and regulations — which they themselves
will choose as important or receive as such from someone

13 But exhort one another daily, while it is called To day; lest any of you be hardened through the deceitfulness of sin.

---

else. When motivated by a lack of trust in the standing Christ makes possible, this too is sinful.

It was this error in part which led to the writing of Galatians (against Judaizing tendencies), Colossians (against an apparently gentile heresy which had adopted rituals and philosophies from many sources), I John (against a budding philosophical heresy later known as gnosticism) and even Hebrews. Christ is sufficient as Savior, and the man who truly has Him has enough. Steadfast faithfulness to Christ is an evidence of this inward faith, and is a necessity if one is to be saved in the end. That is the point of this chapter.

3:13. So that Christians will not fall through unbelief, they are admonished to **exhort** or encourage or comfort **one another.** This is to be done **daily, while it is called today.** Such refreshing of the spirit, such rededication to God and to Christ, will prevent one's being **hardened** or calloused **through the deceitfulness** or error **of sin.**

This exhorting is the duty of every Christian. Barnes asks:

> How often do church-members see a fellow-member go astray without any exhortation or admonition. . . . Belonging to the same family; having the same interests in religion; and all suffering when one suffers, why should they not be allowed tenderly and kindly to exhort one another to a holy life?

In a special sense, this exhorting is to be done by the elders or shepherds of the flock, whose chief duty before God is to watch for souls (Hebrews 13:17; see Ezekiel 33: 7-9). Milligan's comments are still appropriate.

> Do not procrastinate, or put off till tomorrow what should be done today. . . . If the members of every congregation of disciples would all watch over one another, not as censors, but as members of the body of Christ, how many errors might be corrected in their incipiency. But . . . how many delinquent Christians are allowed to become hardened in sin, before even the Elders of the Church call on them and admonish them! How very unlike these Elders are to the Good Shepherd that careth for the sheep.

While such exhorting is to be done daily, it is one pur-

14   For we are made partakers of Christ, if we hold
the beginning of our confidence steadfast unto the end;

15   While it is said, To day if ye will hear his voice,
harden not your hearts, as in the provocation.

16   For some, when they had heard, did provoke:
howbeit not all that came out of Egypt by Moses.

---

pose of the Lord's Day assembly as well. Those who are
absent from the gatherings of the saints fail both to receive
needful exhortation and to contribute their encouragement
to others (Hebrews 10:24-25).

The neglect of Christian exhortation is surely among the
greatest failings of God's people today. The mad rush for
the world's goods, the excessive drive for material prosperi-
ty, the disproportionate love of pleasure, the self-centered
living of a modern age — these all have practically extin-
guished the selfless and obedient concern of saints in too
many places for one another, and the careful exhortation
which should grow out of that concern has died before
it was born. Any congregation that ignores this divine obligation has no right to parade itself as a faithful church of
Christ Jesus, regardless of its other qualities or so-called distinctive marks.

3:14. **We are made partakers** or partners **of Christ** only
if we hold fast **the beginning of our confidence** or grounds
of hope **steadfast unto the end** or conclusion or goal. Our
author addresses his readers in verse one as partakers of the
heavenly calling. But while the call has been issued and
the journey begun, the trip is not completed until its destination is reached. As the Israelites under Moses fell after
they had begun, so Christians will be Christ's partners in
glory only if they are faithful until the conclusion of life
and the attaining of the goal.

3:15. He repeats the admonition from the psalm, this
time with emphasis on the word **provocation.**

3:16. **Some,** after **they had heard, did provoke** God.
This is probably best translated as a question. Who did provoke? The answer is: **all that came out of Egypt by Moses.**

17 But with whom was he grieved forty years? was it not with them that had sinned, whose carcases fell in the wilderness?

18 And to whom sware he that they should not enter into his rest, but to them that believed not?

19 So we see that they could not enter in because of unbelief.

3:17. With whom was he grieved forty years? A few reprobates? No, it was with them that had sinned, whose carcases fell in the wilderness, and that number included the entire company of adults who left Egypt, with the exceptions of Joshua and Caleb. The danger of leaving faith in Christ is grave because the possibility is both real and widespread.

3:18. To whom did God swear that they should not enter into his rest? It was to them that believed not. In this case they had stopped believing although they had begun their journey in faith.

3:19. So we see, he concludes, that they could not enter in because of disbelief. Their death in the wilderness was not due to Moses' unfaithfulness — he was faithful in all God's house. It was not because God was unable to save them — He showed His works forty years in the wilderness. The reason they fell was simple and single: they stopped believing and trusting God. The next verse of exhortation should be included in chapter three: Let us therefore fear, lest, a promise being left us of entering into his rest, any of you should seem to come short of it. It happened once before. It can happen again.

CHAPTER FOUR

The author continues his line of reasoning begun in chapter three. There is no break of thought at this chapter division.

CHAPTER 4

1 Let us therefore fear, lest a promise being left us of entering into his rest, any of you should seem to come short of it.

4:1. Let God's people today **fear** and not fall. This is a real possibility now and was then for the Hebrew Christians or there would be no warning. In the midst of the various and passing issues of each generation, God's people would do well to remember that the fundamental and eternal issue has always been belief versus unbelief and that God (and God alone) will test each individual (as an individual) on that issue. This point should never be forgotten.

The exhortations in Hebrews are rich in edification, and the "let us" admonitions are translated from a verb form called the "hortatory subjunctive" (see 4:11, 14, 16; 6:1; 10:22-24; 12:1, 28; 13:13, 15).

A **promise** has been **left** for us, although the Old Testament saints and apostates have died. That promise concerns **entering into** God's **rest**. The same offer was made the Jews, as our writer explains, but because of disbelief they did not receive the promised blessing. The same offer is now given to believers in Christ. Christians are to fear, however, lest any of them **should seem to come short of it**.

To **come short** might mean to fall short of attaining the promised **rest**, and that point is well taken in this context. But it may also mean to come short of being offered the promise of God in the first place, and the next verses, as well as the verb **should seem**, appear to support this interpretation.

Some of the Hebrew saints appear to have been disappointed in their immediate expectations as Christians. They had given up their ancient religion, they had suffered persecution for their faith, they had endured afflictions for Christ's sake. It seemed to some that all their sacrifices had been in vain. They had not entered into **rest** but into distress. It seemed to some that the promise of a **rest** surely did not apply in their case, for they had not found it. The writer shows that the promise not only does apply to the Christian, but that since it was not fulfilled in the past it must apply to God's people in Christ.

2 For unto us was the gospel preached, as well as unto them: but the word preached did not profit them, not being mixed with faith in them that heard it.

3 For we which have believed do enter into rest, as he said, As I have sworn in my wrath, if they shall enter

---

4:2. God **preached** a **gospel** (good news) to the Jews concerning a promised land. **Unto us** Christians is given good news of present deliverance in Christ and a part in the world to come. The believer is therefore to fear, for the mere fact that he has heard good news does not mean that he will enter into the promise. The Jews also heard good news, yet they died in the wilderness.

The word preached by Moses **did not profit them,** because it was **not mixed with faith in them that heard it.** The figure here is taken from the physical body and the digestive system. The Greek word translated **mixed** was used both of the digestion of food in the stomach and the assimilation of nutrients throughout the body. Regardless of the beauty, taste or value of food, it is of no use to the body unless it is properly digested and assimilated.

The same is true spiritually. Israel heard the word of God but failed to "digest" it through faith and assimilate it to their profit. Food improperly digested will actually do harm. So also the word of God, which is given to save, will be a testimony and assurance of destruction unless it is mixed with faith (II Corinthians 2:15-16). It is not enough to hear God's word. It must be received in faith and held to in patience.

4:3. **We** who **have believed** are the ones who **enter into rest.** Faith is a necessity, as demonstrated by the experience both of those who fell and those who attained. The **rest** into which believers enter (in promise now and in actuality if they persevere) is the same rest of which God spoke in Psalm 95:11, as mentioned already in Hebrews 3:11.

Because God swore **in** His **wrath** that Israel would not enter into His rest, it is evident that (1) He had a rest Himself, and (2) He had planned from the beginning for man to share in it. The quotation is translated correctly in 3:11,

into my rest: although the works were finished from the foundation of the world.

4 For he spake in a certain place of the seventh day on this wise, And God did rest the seventh day from all his works.

5 And in this place again, If they shall enter into my rest.

6 Seeing therefore it remaineth that some must enter therein, and they to whom it was first preached entered not in because of unbelief:

7 Again, he limiteth a certain day, saying in David, To day, after so long a time; as it is said, To day if ye will hear his voice, harden not your hearts.

8 For if Jesus had given them rest, then would he not

---

and should be so worded here. God's **works were finished from the foundation of the world.** Since then He has been in His own rest, and has sought faithful men who would enjoy it with Him.

4:4-5. This is proved by two quotations from Scripture. **God did rest the seventh day from all his works,** according to Genesis 2:2. And then He swore in Psalm 95:11 concerning His rest, saying **if they shall enter** (correctly translated, "they shall surely not enter") **into my** (the pronoun is emphatic) **rest.**

4:6-7. Since it has always been God's intention that **some must enter** into His rest, and since the Jews **to whom it was first preached** did not enter **because of unbelief,** God offered the rest again to those living in the time of David. They were admonished like the Jews in the wilderness to **hear his voice** and **harden not** their **hearts** (Psalm 95:7-8). God's saving time is **today,** whenever that may be. Any day is a day of salvation in which God's word comes to man and is received in faith.

4:8. The fact that the rest was offered to men in the time of David proves that the rest involved was not that found in the land of Canaan. If Joshua (Jesus is the Greek form of the Hebrew name Joshua) **had given them rest** in the land, God **would not afterward have spoken of another day.** Yet He did, as we have just seen.

afterward have spoken of another day.

9 There remaineth therefore a rest to the people of
God.

10 For he that is entered into his rest, he also hath
ceased from his own works, as God did from his.

11 Let us labor therefore to enter into that rest,
lest any man fall after the same example of unbelief.

12 For the word of God is quick, and powerful, and
sharper than any two-edged sword, piercing even to the dividing asunder of soul and spirit, and of the joints and marrow,

---

4:9. The conclusion must be that a rest remains, even
today, for the people of God who will trust in Christ.

4:10. He has not been speaking concerning an ordinary
human rest, which is brief and is followed by more labor.
The man who is entered into God's rest has ceased from
his works forever, just as God did from his at the end of
creation week. This is a rest of accomplished purpose, of
fulfilled action, of completed labor. It is another way of
describing the salvation of 1:14 and 2:3, or the world to
come of 2:5. Because this is the nature of the promised
rest, it is also apparent that the Sabbath rest of the Jews
is not meant, for that was followed by six days of more labor
and had to be repeated every week. In addition, the Sabbath
rest was commanded but this rest of God was always promised (see also Matthew 11:28-30; Revelation 14:13).

4:11. This being the case, all effort is in order to enter
into that rest. Diligence is necessary, because Christians can
fall after the same example of unbelief seen in the Jews
under Moses.

4:12. Diligence is necessary also because of the nature
of the word of God. It is living or quick and energetic or
powerful. It is sharper than any two-edged sword. The figure
continues in saying that the word's fine edge can cut between
soul and spirit, or to the dividing of joints and marrow. The
author is not intending to give a scientific or spiritual analysis of the nature and composition of man. He is stressing the
power and piercing energy of the word of God. God's word

and is a discerner of the thoughts and intents of the heart.

13 Neither is there any creature that is not manifest in his sight: but all things are naked and opened unto the eyes of him with whom we have to do.

14 Seeing then that we have a great high priest, that is passed into the heavens, Jesus the Son of God, let us hold fast our profession.

15 For we have not an high priest which cannot be touched with the feeling of our infirmities; but was in all

_____

is a **discerner of the thoughts and intents of the heart.** Therefore all unbelief will be apparent to God. It is of the utmost importance that His word be received in faith — it is an instrument too dangerous for trifling (see verse two).

4:13. He who knows the heart will not be misled by duplicity or hypocrisy. Nor will He overlook the good and honest heart, though sometimes men do (see John 2:24-25). **All things are naked and opened** before God's eyes. These words may come from either of two sources.

The priest would inspect a sacrifice with care, lest it be blemished; God's scrutiny of the heart is no less meticulous. It is said also that criminals of the first century would sometimes have their head pulled backward on public display, exposing the face to the contempt of general gaze. Nothing in man's heart or life can escape the certain gaze of God — a gaze of disapproval and severity if what He sees is not holy and faithful. But for some there is also a gaze of sympathy and tenderness, as the next verse will show.

4:14. The writer changes his tone from severe warning to gentle appeal. Our high priest carefully searches the heart in total justice, but He is sympathetic to the human condition of His faithful ones when they stumble. **We have a great high priest,** not on earth, but **passed into the heavens.** He is **Jesus the Son of God** — that same Son exalted in chapter one. Because He is our high priest, we are to **hold fast our profession** (see notes at 3:1).

4:15. Christ can **be touched** or, literally, can sympathize, **with** our weaknesses or **the feeling of our infirmities.** He

points tempted like as we are, yet without sin.

16 Let us therefore come boldly unto the throne of grace, that we may obtain mercy, and find grace to help in time of need.

---

has been **tempted,** or put to the test, **in all points like as we are, yet without sin.** Because He was without sin, Christ both saves and judges man. He judges man in presenting His perfect life when man's is so sinful. At the same time He saves man by that perfect life, because He gave it for man's sins, presenting it to the Father in the place of man's. Christ appeared once before God and presented His perfect life as atonement for our sins and as justification for our forgiveness. He will appear a second time to men, without sin, bringing salvation to those who look for Him (9:26, 28; 10:4-18).

4:16. Because we have a sympathetic high priest, one who measures His feelings on the basis of His own experiences as a man, we are exhorted and tenderly encouraged to **come boldly** unto His **throne of grace.** There **we may obtain mercy,** and there we may **find grace to help in** the **time of** our **need.**

Mercy in this verse stands for a Greek word which in the Greek Old Testament represented the Hebrew word for Jehovah's "covenant mercy" or "lovingkindness." Throughout the Old Testament, God demonstrated this lovingkindness in acts of deliverance and grace. The same word described the mercy the people of the covenant were to show each other as joint recipients of Jehovah's covenant-mercy.

Psalm 136 is a psalm of praise for God's covenant-mercy, and it illustrates the many forms it might take. A complete concordance or book of word studies will give many wonderful insights into this concept from the Old Testament. Christians receive the same kind of covenant kindness, mercy, and steadfast love through their union with Jesus Christ.

CHAPTER FIVE

The author has spoken several times already in this epistle concerning Christ as a priest. Christ is our priest

CHAPTER 5

1 For every high priest taken from among men is ordained for men in things pertaining to God, that he may

---

because He has purged our sins — that is part of His more excellent name (1:3). In this He was the sin-offering as well as the administrating officer (2:9). His identification with His people is seen not only in His tasting death for all men but also in His being made like them in all respects. Because Christ has suffered and been tempted, He is a merciful and faithful high priest, able to help those who are tempted (2:17-18).

As high priest, Christ is faithful to God as well as sympathetic to man. In this He is like Moses, though by position He is far superior to that man of God (3:1-6). His sacrificial death has been accomplished and Christ is now in heaven. As our great high priest, He sympathizes with our plight and supplies mercy and grace to meet our needs (4:14-16). Chapter five presents Christ once more as priest, this time in terms of His divine appointment, and with a word of introduction to the particular kind of priesthood into which He has entered.

5:1. For indicates that what follows is based on the final remarks of chapter four. **Every high priest** in the Jewish order is **taken from among men** and is a man himself. The high priest's ministry involves both God and man. He is **ordained** or appointed or divinely named **for** the sake of **men.** That is, he works on their behalf and, we might even say, in their stead. He also serves **in things pertaining to God.** The high priest's central function is making offerings to God **for sins.**

Gifts and sacrifices stand for the total offerings of the high priest to God on behalf of the people (see also 8:3; 9:9). Some have explained **gifts** as non-blood offerings and **sacrifices** as blood offerings. This is not consistent, however, with other passages (Genesis 4:3-4 in the Greek Old Testament, for example) where these words appear with the meanings exactly reversed. A better distinction is made in terms of purpose. **Gifts** are thank-offerings (eucharistic); **sacrifices** are sin-offerings (expiatory). If this is in the au-

offer both gifts and sacrifices for sins:

2   Who can have compassion on the ignorant, and on
them that are out of the way; for that he himself also is
compassed with infirmity.

---

thor's mind, **for sins** modifies only **sacrifices** in the sentence
and not both terms.

5:2. The high priest must be able **to have compassion.**
Literally he "measures his feelings" with the people. He is
not excessively swayed by harsh justice, nor moved overmuch
by indulgent pity. He must measure his feelings in view of
the people's responsibilities on the one hand, but in view
of their circumstances and weaknesses on the other. Himself
a man, he is aware of human weakness. Appointed by God
for divine service, he is aware of God's just and holy demands. The Levitical high priest served in a very exalted
and holy position. His was a representative role: representing God among the people, and representing the people
before God (Exodus 28:29-30, 36-43; see Leviticus 16).

Priestly offerings were for the benefit of **the ignorant,**
that is, those whose sin was unknown to them at the time
they committed it, and for those who were **out of the way,**
which is the literal meaning of erring. The original construction of this verse suggests that both terms refer to the
same people, those who err through ignorance. The point is
that priestly service and offerings were for sins of weakness or ignorance. There was no sacrifice for presumptuous
sins (Numbers 15:30-31; see verses 22ff in the same chapter).
The Hebrews author later gives a similar warning to those
under the new covenant (10:26-29).

It was necessary for the priest to be compassionate,
for he also was **compassed** or surrounded **with infirmity** or
weakness. A play on the word may be intended here, for
the same word which means "surrounded" at other times
means "clothed." The priest was separated from his fellow
Jews and was distinguished from them by the holy robes
of his office. Yet he was one of them in weakness and sin.
Here was an imperfection of the Old Testament priesthood
—the priest, like every other man, was clothed in weakness.
The fact that he also wore priestly robes did not change

3 And by reason hereof he ought, as for the people, so also for himself, to offer for sins.

4 And no man taketh this honor unto himself, but he that is called of God, as was Aaron.

5 So also Christ glorified not himself to be made an high priest; but he that said unto him, Thou art my Son, today have I begotten thee.

---

that! It remained for Christ to serve as perfect priest through His own sinlessness and to offer a perfect sacrifice which could remove sins forever.

5:3. The Levitical priest was obligated **to offer** a sacrifice **for himself** as well as one **for the people.** Though he was called by God and was appointed to a sacred office, he was still a sinner himself.

5:4. **No man** among the Jews took the priesthood to **himself.** The priests were appointed of God, as signified in the divine appointment of **Aaron** their head (Exodus 28:1).

5:5. Nor did **Christ** glorify **himself** by taking the office of **high priest** presumptuously, but He was so honored or glorified by God the Father. Two Messianic psalms are quoted here and applied to Jesus Christ as Son and priest. The first is Psalm 2:7, which was used to prove Christ's Sonship in 1:5 (see the notes there on this quotation).

5:6. The second quotation is from Psalm 110:4, and will figure prominently in the discussion of the next two chapters of Hebrews. As Psalm two joined the position of Son to that of King, so Psalm 110 related the functions of King and Priest. By using both these passages, the writer shows Christ to be Son (which in chapter one had the significance of Prophet), Priest (which he is about to discuss) and King. Our author used the first verse of Psalm 110 in 1:13 and in the verses now following he will discuss verse four of that psalm.

God said to Christ in His resurrection, "Thou art my Son, this day have I begotten thee" (Acts 13:33). At the same time, according to the present passage, He constituted Him high priest. Here the emphasis will be on the eternal

**6 As he saith also in another place, Thou art a priest
for ever after the order of Melchizedek.**

7 Who in the days of his flesh, when he had offered

---

nature of Christ's priesthood ("thou art a priest forever");
Acts 13 also stresses Christ's unending life (verses 34-37).
Here the eternal priesthood of Christ means continual salvation for His people (7:23-25); the "therefore" of Acts
13:38 shows the same consequential blessing.

Aaron was not only called of God (Exodus 28:1), he
was also confirmed as God's chosen one by a miracle of new
life. When Korah, Dathan and Abiram questioned Aaron's
authority and office (Numbers 16:1-3), the ground opened
beneath them and their families, swallowing them alive, and
a fire from God consumed their followers (verses 31-35). God
then confirmed Aaron's appointment by making his rod
(a piece of dead wood) come to life again, bear buds, bloom
blossoms and yield almonds (Numbers 17).

Christ was called by God to be high priest. He, too, was
confirmed by a miracle of new life. His dead body, wrapped
in burial clothes and entombed for three days, was given
life by the power of God. He now lives to make priestly intercession for His people, through the merits of His own
sacrificial blood.

Woe to any person who questions Christ's divine appointment or loses confidence in His sacred work of redemption!
The "gainsaying of Korah" is still a present danger (Jude
11). The first readers of Hebrews were urged to put their
confidence in Christ as God's appointed high priest —
divinely-appointed, all-sufficient and everlasting. That exhortation is no less needful today among those claiming to
follow Him.

5:7. **Who** refers to Christ, not Melchizedek. **In the days
of his flesh** refers to the earthly life of Christ in a
human body. It is the time of His flesh and blood (2:14)
when He partook of the seed of Abraham (2:16). This was
the time in which He was in all points tempted (4:15).

Chapter ten will detail the significance of Christ's
fleshly body. Here the intent is to demonstrate what was

**up prayers and supplications with strong crying and tears
unto him that was able to save him from death, and was**

stated in verse five: Christ did not take the office of high
priest to Himself but was given the position by God. It was
not attained by arrogant assumption but by obedient suffering. Suffering and obedience are joined in the verses which
follow and together are related to salvation, first in the life
of Christ and then in the lives of those He saves.

Four terms express the intensity of Christ's suffering
in the face of death. **Prayers** signify pleadings or beggings,
with reference to a need. **Supplications** stress the act of im-
ploring or asking. **Strong crying** shows the depth of these
calls for help. **Tears** are not mentioned in the Gospel accounts of Gethsemane, but were certainly visible on that
occasion as an external indication of the utter agony of soul
within the Lord (Matthew 26:36-44; Mark 14:32-41; Luke
22:39-45).

These prayers were offered to **him that was able to save
him from death,** that is, the Father (see notes at 2:12-13).
Some commentators see two prayers here: that God would
save Christ from death on the cross, or that He would
save Him from death by resurrection if the first prayer was
not answered. Lenski correctly notes that Jesus is nowhere
pictured as praying for the resurrection. On that basis he argues strongly for the first sense only. God was able to save
the Son from the cross — by twelve legions of angels, if
necessary (Matthew 26:53). But it was not the Father's will
to do that, nor was it in accord with the Scriptures, as Jesus
Himself had pointed out to His disciples (Matthew 26:54).

The statement that Christ **was heard** in these prayers is
confusing to some, but need not be when thought is given
to the actual prayer of the Lord. Christ did not pray simply
that the cup of suffering might pass Him by, though that
was included in His request (see references above). His primary prayer — and this is the writer's chief point in this
verse — was for the will of God to be done! That prayer
was answered — by the death, yes, and by the resurrection
of the Son who willingly submitted to the Father's sovereign
will! See the references given above, also John 12:23-33.
Again there may be an allusion to Psalm 22, where the

heard in that he feared;

8 Though he were a Son, yet learned he obedience

---

speaker cries to God (verse two) and is heard (verse 24). See the comments at 2:12 on that psalm.

Christ was heard **in that he feared.** Literally the text says, "because of (His) reverent fear" or "fearful reverence." "If it be possible, let this cup pass from me," prayed the Savior, with strong crying and tears. But with the same intensity He respectfully and fearfully climaxed that prayer, "nevertheless, not my will, but thine be done!"

We are dealing here with the perfect obedience of the Son of God. This is an obedience unto death, an obedience perfected only in suffering. In the face of such absolute dedication to God's will — and that at the cost of all personal claims and human ambitions or even life — in the face of this divine obedience angels weep, demons shudder and sinful man must cry out in abject remorse, "God, be merciful to me, a sinner!"

How inadequate all our obedience is in this light! How meagre our dedication to the Father's will! How far short of God's glory and the Savior's example we see our own self-willed lives! Our Lord did not presume anything of His own accord. He did not hold back anything in His obedience and submission to the Father's perfect will. With every ounce of His deepest feeling He threw Himself in His Father's arms, there to depend on the Father's strength as He exclaimed simply, "Thy will be done!"

5:8. Yet being the **Son** — that more excellent Son of chapter one — Christ **learned obedience.** The Greek here says "the" obedience, as if to underscore the thought. Christ **learned** obedience in experiencing absolute submission to God's will. This does not mean that His life ever contained any element of rebellion or disobedience, for it did not. He came for the purpose of doing God's will (Hebrews 10:7) and He finished what He came to do (John 17:4).

Learned here translates rather a word kin to that from which we have "disciple" and "discipline." Christ was the disciple, par excellence. He experienced the full discipline

by the things which he suffered;

**9 And being made perfect, he became the author of
eternal salvation unto all them that obey him;**

---

of obedience — even in suffering. By His suffering He
learned experientially what full obedience means. In this
He learned and qualified to sanctify those who should put
their trust in Him. He is now perfectly able to help them
when they are tempted (see 2:17-18).

5:9. Christ was **made perfect**, not in a moral sense, but
for the business of saving. **He** then **became the author** or
source **of eternal salvation unto all them that obey him.**
By the obedience learned only in suffering, Christ was
made complete as Captain of salvation (2:10). By the same
suffering and obedience He was perfected as Source of
eternal salvation. "Captain" signifies "pioneer," and Christ
has already gone ahead to enter the eternal glory which will
be shared one day by the "many sons" (2:10; see 6:20).

Author here means "source," as it is only from Christ,
and through Him, and by His work of obedience that those
"sons" will share in the glory He now has as Son. **Author**
may also be translated "cause," suggesting that Christ's perfect obedience is the cause of our salvation, not our own
imperfect obedience, though this very verse affirms the
fact of obedience on our part if we are recipients of the
salvation He has made a reality. The English connection
between "author" and "authority" is not in our word here,
though Christ certainly has all authority as Son and Lord
(Matthew 28:18; Philippians 2:9-11).

Christ is author or cause or source of salvation **to them
that obey him.** It is always the case that blessing follows
obedience, though sometimes the obedience of one man
secures blessing for another. Abraham's obedience was
the basis on which God blessed his descendants (Genesis
22:15-18; Deuteronomy 4:37; 9:4-6). How much more does
Christ's obedience — a perfect obedience — result in the
perfect salvation of all who share sonship with Him (see
Romans 5:19). Yet those who share Christ's sonship and
His righteousness (Isaiah 61:9-11; Jeremiah 23:5-6; 33:15-16;
I Corinthians 1:30; II Corinthians 5:21; Philippians 3:9) must

10 Called of God an high priest after the order of Melchizedek.

11 Of whom we have many things to say, and hard to be uttered, seeing ye are dull of hearing.

---

and will share also with Him in faithful obedience to God — an obedience in which He led the way, set the example and obtained salvation for those who follow.

5:10. Because Christ did not glorify Himself to be made a high priest (verse five), choosing instead the submissiveness of suffering, He was **called** or greeted by God as **high priest after the order of Melchizedek.** Melchizedek held the double office of priest-king, a privilege denied the priestly offspring of Levi or the royal heirs of Judah — that is, until Christ came. Now He, the prophet-Son, serves also as high priest and as king.

5:11. Having introduced Melchizedek, our author immediately leaves him for the moment. He attributes this digression in thought to the dullness of his hearers. After a warning and exhortation in chapter six, he will return to a detailed analysis of Melchizedek's priesthood in chapter seven. There he will show Melchizedek's office to be unlike that of Aaron's sons, but of the same sort as the Son's which it prefigures.

We have many things to say is literally "the discourse or conversation is much or long." **Hard to be uttered** does not mean that the writer had difficulty expressing himself, but that his discourse concerning Melchizedek would be interpreted or explained only with elaboration, for which his readers were not prepared. The transmitter was working well but the receivers needed repairs!

Dull of hearing is literally "sluggish or numb in ears (hearing)." Lenski remarks: "Unbelief closes the ears; incipient unbelief dulls them." These readers had not fallen into apostate unbelief but were apparently drifting in that direction. Our author pauses long enough to point this out to them and to sharpen their dull ears.

12 For when for the time ye ought to be teachers, ye have need that one teach you again which be the first principles of the oracles of God; and are become such as have need of milk, and not of strong meat.

5:12. **For** indicates the cause of his statement. With reference to **the time** which has passed since they became Christians, his readers should have become **teachers.** The word here indicates clock-time, not merely "occasion" (as in Romans 13:11 and other places).

Rather than this, however, they still had **need** for someone to **teach** them **again.** It is not in difficult matters alone that they are ignorant. They need instruction in **first principles,** the rudimentary matters, the spiritual ABC's.

How well this indictment fits so many in the church today. How many there are now who should have been teaching others long ago yet who continually need teaching in elementary principles. Some people are simply dull of hearing; others are "ever learning and never able to come to the knowledge of the truth" (II Timothy 3:7). The first need to be sharpened; the second are to be rejected (II Timothy 3:5). The recipients of Hebrews were at the first point but not yet to the second.

They were in need of **milk,** not **strong meat** or solid food. Milk is a predigested food, suited for one who lacks ability to receive and digest his own nourishment. The spiritual milk-baby is not able to learn and digest his own spiritual food. He depends on someone else to do most of his learning and thinking for him. This is a beginning point, to be sure, but it should not characterize those who **for the time** ought to be able to teach others.

A certain measure of the blame for this condition must be put on some among the teachers and preachers who have not led the babes to stronger food. When the bottle is administered at every feeding time, and often the same formula warmed over, the hungry souls can not be expected to develop into maturity. Let each teacher and preacher learn from this context as well, to follow our author's example as he himself leaves the **first principles** to carry his readers on to maturity and perfection.

13 For every one that useth milk is unskillful in the word of righteousness: for he is a babe.

14 But strong meat belongeth to them that are of full age, even those who by reason of use have their senses exercised to discern both good and evil.

CHAPTER 6

1 Therefore leaving the principles of the doctrine

5:13. The spiritual infant who still partakes milk is **unskillful** or inexperienced **in the word of righteousness.** As an infant is without experience in eating strong food so long as he remains with milk alone, so the believer who never has experience in teaching others will remain in need of simple nourishment himself. This is not condoned but condemned.

5:14. **Strong meat** is for the one who is of **full age,** the perfect or mature person. The mature Christian **by reason of use** or exercise has his **senses exercised to discern both good and evil.**

Senses translates a word which gives our "aesthetics," though here it has a figurative meaning. **Exercised** is from a word family which gives "gymnasium," and suggests perhaps that maturity in spiritual discernment comes only through regular workouts.

To discern good and evil represents the ability and/or the authority to make independent moral choices (see Genesis 3:5, 22; Deuteronomy 1:39; II Samuel 14:17; 19:35; I Kings 3:9; Isaiah 7:16). The Christian is to mature to the point of making his own moral judgments; he is to learn to discern the Lord's will in each circumstance of his own life (see Romans 12:2; Ephesians 5:10, 17; I Thessalonians 4:1-4).

CHAPTER SIX

6:1. **The principles of the doctrine of Christ** are the elementary matters which had been previously taught to the Hebrew Christians. They are encouraged to be **leaving** these things — not in the sense of rejecting their truthful-

**of Christ, let us go on unto perfection; not laying again the
foundation of repentance from dead works, and of faith**

---

ness, or attempting to unlearn them, but as a child leaves the
first reader in school for one more advanced, or as he
leaves milk for solid nourishment. And they are called to
go on to perfection or maturity or completion. The idea of
perfection will reappear in the coming chapters.

It is necessary to lay a **foundation** in the construction
of a firm building, but once the foundation has been laid, it
is not put down again and again. This point is the basis for
verses four through six. Those who fall away, having once
been instructed in the fundamentals, will not be reclaimed
by beginning from the first as if they had never heard the
gospel. If they experienced these initial responses and
understood these fundamentals — but then fell away —
they have rejected what they know and have no room in
their hearts for a conversion as at the first. **Again** is an
important word in understanding these verses.

Six matters are listed as elementary principles, and
they have been variously interpreted. Some take these as
elements of Old Testament teaching in contrast to the more
perfect lessons of the gospel. It is true that the terms which
follow are all used at times of elements of pre-Christian
truth. On the other hand, it seems more nearly correct to
think of these fundamentals as basics in Christian instruction, both in view of the larger context and the specific
terms as well.

The six points are given in three pairs of two each.
We might speak of these pairs under the headings of preparation, initiation and motivation or direction. First mentioned is **repentance from dead works** and **faith toward
God.** Repentance and faith are joined also in Mark 1:15 and
Acts 20:21. In repentance, one feels the guilt of his own
sin and rebellion against God, is sorry for it, and purposes
to change his direction of life. He abandons **dead works** (see
9:14), "works of righteousness" or "works of law," which
are **dead** because they lead to death, can not bring spiritual
life and are futile so far as pleasing God. Someone has
pictured works springing from obligation as dead in the
sense that they do not spring from life. They are as sheep's

toward God,

**2   Of the doctrine of baptisms, and of laying on of
hands, and of resurrection of the dead, and of eternal judgment.**

---

wool draped over a wolf's back; there is no vital connection
between the animal and the wool.

In **faith toward God** one not only accepts intellectually
that God is, but places his confidence in God for salvation.
He does this by trusting the reconciliation God has already
brought about through the life and death of Jesus Christ,
and by throwing himself on the mercy and grace of God by
identification with that sinless Son through living faith.

By repentance, man denies himself; by faith, he takes
up his cross to follow Jesus. By repentance, he is crucified
to the old way of life and all human merit or personal
boasting; by faith, he takes hold of life in Christ and gratefully claims the merit and reward of Christ's perfect life.
Repentance and **faith** here stand for the initial hearing of
the gospel and the response of the heart to it.

6:2. The next pair consists of **the doctrine** or teaching
of baptisms and of **the laying on of hands.** The word here
translated **baptisms** is that commonly applied to the various
washings of the Old Testament (see 9:10; Mark 7:4). The
doctrine of baptisms would therefore seem to involve explanations regarding the difference between Jewish washings on the one hand and gospel baptism in the name of
Jesus the Messiah on the other. This would certainly involve
some teaching on the significance of Christ's blood and
sacrifice, a point to be developed in detail later in the
epistle.

Laying on of hands was done in healing, blessing, or
simply giving approval and endorsement. Many scholars
feel that the laying on of hands also accompanied believer's
baptism and signified the giving of the Holy Spirit. If so,
these two teachings go together in a special way and have
to do with Christian initiation, or entering upon the Christian life.

Resurrection of the dead and **eternal judgment** form the
third pair of fundamental principles, and have to do with

3 And this will we do, if God permit.

4 For it is impossible for those who were once enlightened, and have tasted of the heavenly gift, and were made partakers of the Holy Ghost,

5 And have tasted the good word of God, and the powers of the world to come,

---

Christian motivation or direction. These are not the only proper motives, to be sure, but in the elementary teaching of the gospel one is taught to look to the resurrection and judgment as the completion of what God has already begun, and therefore as motives for faithfulness.

6:3. The writer acknowledges his dependance on the will of God. If God is willing, he will lead the reader to more advanced teaching and so to personal maturity.

6:4. Those who were once enlightened are Christians who have been instructed in the first principles of verses one and two (see also 10:32). The following terms refer to these same individuals. In the post-apostolic writings, "enlightenment" came to be a technical term for baptism. In the New Testament the knowledge of God through Christ in the gospel is put in terms of light (John 1:9; Acts 26:18; Colossians 1:12-13). Once is an important word, and means once for all time. This enlightenment can take place only once; it can not be repeated.

Taste signifies experience (see 2:9). The heavenly gift may mean the Holy Spirit, the remission of sins, or (probably) the entire new life as a child of God. As partaker of the Holy Ghost, Christians are partners of the Spirit. He is God's gift, the seal and earnest of future blessing and the originator of fruit well-pleasing to God (Acts 2:38; 5:32; II Corinthians 1:22; Ephesians 1:13-14; Galatians 5:22-25).

6:5. Those who have tasted the good word of God are those who have experienced fulfillment of the precious promises God offers by claiming and receiving them in faith. The expression used here occurs also in the Greek Old Testament at Zechariah 1:13 and Joshua 21:45. The powers of the world to come probably refer to the miraculous

6 If they shall fall away, to renew them again unto repentance; seeing they crucify to themselves the Son of God afresh, and put him to an open shame.

manifestations given the infant church (see notes at 2:3-4), but to a Jewish Christian this phrase would speak of the present reality of the Messianic era in which such things would take place. **The world to come** is literally the Coming Age, which is how the Jews spoke of the era of fulfillment and blessing under Messiah in the Kingdom of God (see notes at 1:2; see also 1:14; 2:5; 13:14).

6:6. **If** is not in the original Greek, and the verb **fall away** is of the same tense as those preceding it in verses four and five. It is impossible **to renew again unto repentance** those who experienced the benefits of verses four and five, then **fell away** (our almost-literal English idiom would be "dropped out"). Not that all hope is gone, for God may once again give them repentance in acknowledging the truth (II Timothy 2:25). But it is impossible for those individuals to experience again the renewal through enlightenment which was theirs in the first hearing of the gospel (see Acts 11:18). They can not **again** go through the fundamental process of repentance and faith, or of initiation into the body of Christ, as they did before (read this verse in the context of those preceding it). They have done that once, but have now rejected all that God offers. For such a person the gospel holds no appeal.

These individuals (considered hypothetically as among the readers) **crucify** for **themselves the Son of God.** By their apostasy they judge Christ to be an imposter and guilty of death. In such a person repentance cannot take place, for it is based on godly sorrow and a conviction of sin growing out of faith in Christ as the Son of God.

Such apostates **put** Christ **to an open shame** (see 10:29). This same verb is used in the Greek Old Testament at Numbers 25:4 ("hang them up," KJV), where its point is clearly seen in a context of apostasy from God. Christians who fall away do just this to the Son of God. They hang Him on the cross again, whether they forsake Christ for the world, for antichrist religion, or simply for carelessness and indifference.

7   For the earth which drinketh in the rain that cometh
oft upon it, and bringeth forth herbs meet for them by
whom it is dressed, receiveth blessing from God:

8   But that which beareth thorns and briers is rejected, and is nigh unto cursing; whose end is to be burned.

9   But, beloved, we are persuaded better things of you,
and things that accompany salvation, though we thus speak.

10   For God is not unrighteous to forget your work and
labor of love, which ye have showed toward his name, in
that ye have ministered to the saints, and do minister.

6:7-8. **The earth** or ground **which drinketh in the rain**
and then bears produce **meet** or fitting and appropriate for
those who have worked, **receiveth blessing from God.** On the
other hand ground which produces **thorns and briers** or
thistles proves itself unworthy of blessing and is rejected
(the same word translated "reprobate" in II Corinthians
13:5-7) for cultivation. Instead it is burned over, perhaps
to prevent the further spread of briers to the adjoining land.
A double meaning is certainly intended here, for such un-
productive and evil men will meet their **end** in the **burning**
of hell (see a similar thought in Matthew 3:10, 12; 13:30;
John 15:6).

6:9. What is true in the physical realm is true also in
the spiritual, and the author's intention is to prevent this
fate among his readers. Having given such a stern warning,
he now quickly softens his tone to encouragement. He is
persuaded or convinced that **better things** than this will
come from his readers. He looks for the fruitful lives and
works which **accompany salvation,** things closely aligned with
it and holding fast to it (see Ephesians 2:10; other passages
in notes on 13:21). His words are meant as a warning, not
as a present judgment. His readers have shown fruits worthy
of God in the past, and he urges them to remain steadfast
in such a life in the future.

6:10. **God is not unrighteous** and will not **forget** any
work or **labor** growing out of **love** and done because of **his**
name or because of the relationship sustained to Him. The
Hebrew Christians had **ministered to** or served **the saints,**
their brethren — both in the past and in the writer's present
(see 10:32-34).

11 And we desire that every one of you do show the
same diligence to the full assurance of hope unto the end:

12 That ye be not slothful, but followers of them who
through faith and patience inherit the promises.

13 For when God made promise to Abraham, because
he could swear by no greater, he sware by himself,

14 Saying, Surely blessing I will bless thee, and mul-
tiplying I will multiply thee.

15 And so, after he had patiently endured, he obtained the promise.

6:11. He wants **every one** of them to demonstrate the
same diligence, not only now but **to the full assurance of hope
unto the end.** Their danger was in stopping short of completion, of falling back before the goal had been attained.
Against this he warns repeatedly (3:6, 14; 10:23).

6:12. They are not to be **slothful** (the same word translated "dull" in 5:11; see notes there), but rather are to be
(literally "become") **followers** or imitators of those godly
men of old who did **inherit** the blessings contained in
God's **promises.** Success always comes **through faith** (which
in the Bible means trust, reliance and commitment as well as
intellectual acceptance) **and patience** or longsuffering perseverance.

6:13. **For** example, **when God** promised **Abraham** in
Genesis 22:16-18 concerning his numerous descendants and
other blessings, God **could swear by no greater** person than
Himself, and so **he sware by** His own name or personal
character.

6:14. In the Hebrew text of this passage, an idiom is
used which simply means "I will surely bless you and multiply you." The Greek Old Testament translated the phrase
word for word and gave the rather awkward reading which
our author quotes here and which is carried over into the
English.

6:15. **So,** thus, in this manner and under these circumstances, Abraham first **patiently endured;** only then **he
obtained** the fulfillment of the **promise.** He saw the beginning of the fulfillment in the spared life of Isaac. The rest

16 For men verily swear by the greater: and an oath for confirmation is to them an end of all strife.

17 Wherein God, willing more abundantly to show unto the heirs of promise the immutability of his counsel, confirmed it by an oath:

18 That by two immutable things, in which it was impossible for God to lie, we might have a strong consolation, who have fled for refuge to lay hold upon the hope set before us:

19 Which hope we have as an anchor of the soul, both

---

he saw only by faith according to 11:13, 39. As Abraham had to wait, so do we. This is the writer's exhortation, and this is why he mentions Abraham.

6:16. It is the case with **men** to **swear by the greater** than themselves. Among men, **an oath** serves two purposes. Negatively, it is **an end of all strife.** When a man takes an oath there is no more point in disputing his word or questioning him. Positively, it is **for confirmation.** It gives all the assurance that is possible by the spoken word.

6:17. Because of this, God condescended to man's own level of understanding and **confirmed** His promise to Abraham **by an oath.** This was to **show** or demonstrate to **the heirs of promise** (see 1:14; 9:15) the unchangeableness or **immutability** of God's **counsel** or purpose and design.

6:18. God's promise was made twice sure **by two immutable things:** His word (it is **impossible for God to lie**), and His oath (taken in His own name). As man views the situation, he may have full confidence in the promise of God.

Strong is emphatic here and is read by weak men who need the encouragement. **Consolation** would be better translated "encouragement." Christians are those who **have fled for refuge** (the Greek Old Testament uses the same word of fleeing to the cities of refuge). **The hope set before us** is to be laid hold of or seized. God's twice-sure word of promise is a strong encouragement for all Christians, by patient waiting, to do just that.

6:19. This hope is **an anchor of the soul.** The anchor was a symbol of hope in the ancient world as well as now.

sure and steadfast, and which entereth into that within the
veil;

20 Whither the forerunner is for us entered, even
Jesus, made an high priest for ever after the order of
Melchizedek.

Our anchor is both sure or unfailing and steadfast or firmly fixed.We can have strong confidence in our hope. Within
the veil indicates the most holy place of the tabernacle, into which only the high priest entered one day each year.
The phrase here symbolizes the presence of God, and refers
to the fact that Jesus has passed into heaven as the next
verse will state.

6:20. Into the very presence of God in heaven our
forerunner has already entered (see 2:9-10; 4:14). Forerunner in secular Greek was used of a scout, one who went
before and led the way (see notes on "author" at 5:9).
Jesus has not only entered into God's presence for us
(though as high priest He did that); He has also entered
into heaven in front of us — leading the way and guaranteeing by His own entrance that the path is clear for us to
follow.

The Christian's hope is certain and confident. It is
grounded in the person of Jesus Christ and is based on His
sinless life and His atoning death. If our hope were in our
own obedience or knowledge or power, we could have no
strong confidence at all. But it rests in the Son of God, and
for that reason it is sinful not to have strong confidence.

The Christian's sin is no cause for loss of hope, but
rather for genuine repentance and prayer — for throwing
himself on the mercies of God through his mediator Jesus
Christ. Because of the life Jesus lived and the death He died
— and because the Christian is one with Him — God's people ought to cherish a living hope. They have fled for
refuge to the merciful and all-powerful Son of God. Nor do
they wait for the death of a high priest, for Jesus is their
high priest, and He lives forever — after the order of
Melchizedek.

CHAPTER 7

1 For this Melchizedek, king of Salem, priest of the most high God, who met Abraham returning from the slaughter of the kings, and blessed him;

CHAPTER SEVEN

Having introduced Melchizedek in 5:10-11, our author temporarily put him aside to give in chapter six an exhortation to diligence and steadfastness and a warning regarding the end of slothfulness. He then returned in 6:20 to Melchizedek. Now he discusses him at length in chapter seven, which follows.

7:1. This Melchizedek was the subject of much speculation in Jewish circles, including the Essene community of the Qumran Dead Sea Scrolls. He is mentioned in Scripture, however, only in Hebrews, Psalm 110 and Genesis 14. Melchizedek was a king-priest, contemporary of Abraham, and a servant of God. Salem is probably an ancient name for Jerusalem (see Psalm 76:2). Adoni-zedek, another Old Testament king of Jerusalem (Joshua 10:1), had the same element in his name as Melchi-zedek, which also indicates an identification of Salem with Jerusalem. Some have suggested that Salem here is the Salim of John 3:23; a few take the term figuratively as a title (see verse two) devoid of any geographical intent. It is in line with known facts to suppose that Melchizedek was an actual priest-king of the city-state captured by David from the Jebusites and known to us as Jerusalem (see comments at 12:22).

Melchizedek is **priest of the most high God,** and this point interests our author. Although the Hebrew term parallels the name of a Canaanite god, there is no reason to think that Melchizedek served any deity other than Jehovah. The Most High God is identified in Genesis as the God of Abraham; the Greek Old Testament lies behind the phrase in our present passage; Old and New Testament writers alike present Melchizedek as a servant of Jehovah.

Genesis 14:17-20 reports that Melchizedek **met Abraham** as he was **returning from the slaughter of the kings**

2 To whom also Abraham gave a tenth part of all; first being by interpretation King of righteousness, and after that also King of Salem, which is, King of peace;

---

of the East who had taken Lot captive in the course of a plundering campaign. That text also says that Melchizedek **blessed** Abraham, a point our author will consider later.

7:2. Abraham gave a tenth part or tithe **of all** that he had to Melchizedek. Melchizedek's name is now analyzed in its separate Hebrew components. This practice, though strange by Western logic, was not an uncommon method of reasoning when Hebrews was written — and here it has the approval of the Holy Spirit. The name Melchizedek is composed of two Hebrew words; **melek** means "king" and **tsedek** means "righteousness." Together they mean **king of righteousness,** which, **by interpretation,** Melchizedek was. He is also called **King of Salem,** and since Salem stands for the Hebrew **shalom** or "peace," Melchizedek is here called **king of peace.**

Righteousness and peace appear together frequently in the Old Testament Scriptures (see for example Psalm 72:7; Isaiah 9:6-7; Zechariah 9:9-10). To the Hebrew, "righteousness" meant the faithful performing of all duties proper to a relationship. In a spiritual sense that meant faithfulness to God first of all, because of His covenant mercies to Israel, then faithfulness to fellow-Jews who were recipients of the same covenant blessings.

In Isaiah 5:7, God looks among His people for righteousness but finds instead a cry. The cry speaks of perverted justice, cruelty and a general absence of the life described by righteousness. There is also a play on words in the Hebrew text of this verse, but that does not concern us here.

When the people maintained righteousness, "peace" was the result. Again the term has first a spiritual significance of peace with God, and then of peace with one's fellows under God's covenant care and rule. There could be no peace apart from righteousness, and righteousness was expected to result in peace (Isaiah 32:17). Melchizedek of Salem incorporated both these concepts in his name and office, and even in this foreshadowed the Lord who is our

3 Without father, without mother, without descent, having neither beginning of days, nor end of life; but made like unto the Son of God; abideth a priest continually.

4 Now consider how great this man was, unto whom even the patriarch Abraham gave the tenth of the spoils.

Righteousness and our Peace (I Corinthians 1:30; Ephesians 2:14).

7:3. Melchizedek had no ancestor in the priesthood. Unlike the Jewish priests who had to establish their genealogy to qualify for service (Nehemiah 7:63-64; Leviticus 21: 17; Ezekiel 44:22), this man neither received his office by hereditary right nor passed it on to a physical descendant. So far as we are told in Scripture, he was without father or mother; not that he was other than human, but that he did not belong to any line of priests.

Without descent is better translated "without genealogy." See the point just above. Neither beginning of days nor end of life means that Melchizedek's priesthood is not recorded as to origin or end. He is a lone figure who suddenly appears on the stage of history for a brief moment, then as suddenly and mysteriously removes from the scene. No one can say of this strange man, "here is the beginning of his priestly service" or "here is the end of his priesthood."

Because God opened the curtain in the middle of Melchizedek's priestly service and closed it in the same place, Melchizedek is made like unto the Son of God, who is also alone in a unique priesthood. Continually is not the phrase usually translated "forever," but may be translated "for the duration," "perpetually," or "without interruption." This term will appear later in the chapter.

7:4. In the following verses we will consider how great Melchizedek was. In the first place, Abraham — not another by the same name, but the patriarch himself — paid tithes to Melchizedek. Nor was this a poor tithe, but of the spoils, literally "off the top of the heap" — the choicest tenth.

5   And verily they that are of the sons of Levi, who
receive the office of the priesthood, have a commandment
to take tithes of the people according to the law, that is,
of their brethren, though they come out of the loins of
Abraham:

6   But he whose descent is not counted from them received tithes of Abraham, and blessed him that had the
promises.

7   And without all contradiction the less is blessed of
the better.

8   And here men that die receive tithes; but there he
receiveth them, of whom it is witnessed that he liveth.

9   And as I may so say, Levi also, who receiveth tithes,
paid tithes in Abraham.

7:5. The sons of Levi or the Levitical priests, who receive
the office they hold, take tithes because of a commandment
and a law. They also take tithes from their own brethren,
who are descendants of Abraham.

7:6. Melchizedek is one whose descent is not from
them, who had no commandments or law requiring Abraham to pay him tithes, and who had not received his priesthood by virtue of a lineage. Yet he received tithes, and
that not from just any passing stranger, but from Abraham!
To this add the fact that Melchizedek then blessed Abraham
— the Abraham who had the promises from God.

7:7. It is indisputable that the less is blessed in this
sense by the better. If Abraham was blessed by Melchizedek,
it follows that Melchizedek was a "better" man in terms of
rank and office than the patriarch. Both men acknowledged
this relative position: Abraham, by paying tithes to Melchizedek; Melchizedek, by blessing Abraham.

7:8. By comparison, note also that here in the Levitical
priesthood men that die receive tithes (see I Chronicles
6:49-53), but there in Melchizedek's case one received them
who had no successor.

7:9. To cap it all, and to be perfectly truthful about it,
Levi also, who receiveth tithes under the law from his
Jewish brethren, there paid tithes instead, in Abraham.

10 For he was yet in the loins of his father, when Melchizedek met him.

11 If therefore perfection were by the Levitical priesthood, (for under it the people received the law,) what further need was there that another priest should rise after the order of Melchizedek, and not be called after the order of Aaron?

7:10. If one objects that Levi was not present in Genesis 14, the writer notes that he was yet in the loins of his father Abraham when Melchizedek met him. Just as he can say that Levi received tithes (in the person of his descendants), so he can say as well that Levi paid tithes (in the person of his ancestor). Levi was forefather of the priestly tribe; therefore Melchizedek's priesthood was greater than Aaron's.

Our author has dealt with Melchizedek's characteristics as a person (verses one through three) and in relation to the Levitical priests (verses four through ten). Now he turns to his primary point, an exaltation of the priesthood of Christ in comparison with the Old Testament Jewish priesthood. Verses 11-14 show that the priesthood was the basis of the law, and that because Christ's priesthood after the order of Melchizedek is permanent, so is the law which rests upon it. This is in contrast with the priesthood of Aaron, for it changed, necessitating a change in the law related to it.

7:11. If perfection (a key word in Hebrews; consult a concordance) were by the Levitical priesthood, there would have been no further need for another priest after another order — that of Melchizedek and not of Aaron. An institution is perfect when it accomplishes the purpose for which it was instituted. The Aaronic priesthood did not do that.

The purpose of a priesthood is to bring men to God, to atone for their sins. The author will show clearly in the following chapters that the Levitical sacrifices and priesthood could not do this — either perfectly or permanently. In the present passage, then, he refers to this imperfection in the Old Testament priestly order. He also shows that it had to be replaced by a perfect order which could fulfill these purposes.

12 For the priesthood being changed, there is made of necessity a change also of the law.

13 For he of whom these things are spoken pertaineth to another tribe, of which no man gave attendance at the altar.

14 For it is evident that our Lord sprang out of Judah; of which tribe Moses spake nothing concerning priesthood.

We are accustomed to thinking of the priesthood as dependent on the law. Our author says the opposite. The law depended on the priesthood. This suggests that in God's ordering of affairs the priesthood was first in importance, then the law. Law pointed men to the reality of sin and to the fact that they were sinners. This recognition called for the priesthood as the divine ordinance and institution for the removal of sins. But the imperfection of the Old Testament priesthood pointed them even further to the future when the Son of God would come as great high priest and Lamb of God, completely removing all sins forever by one offering of Himself. The priesthood, then, was the basis and grounds of the law.

7:12. When the priesthood was changed, there was of necessity a change also of the law. When the foundation is removed the building collapses. There can be no legal code unless there is provision for those who break it. In the case of Israel, the priesthood is changed (to one which is perfect), then a new law is given based on that perfect priesthood and relating to it. There is room for thought along this line, that the new law (perfectly suited to its priesthood) is as far superior in nature as well as content to the old, as the new priesthood of Christ is superior to the priesthood of Aaron's sons. The purpose of each law is suited to its particular priesthood.

7:13. He of whom these things are spoken is the Lord Jesus Christ, as the next verse will state, and He belongs to another or a different tribe from Levi. He is of a tribe from which no man ever served at the priestly altar.

7:14. It is evident on the basis of His genealogies in Matthew chapter one and Luke chapter three that our Lord descended from Judah, a tribe from which the Law of

15 And it is yet far more evident: for that after the similitude of Melchizedek there ariseth another priest,

16 Who is made, not after the law of a carnal commandment, but after the power of an endless life.

Moses said absolutely **nothing** so far as **priesthood** is concerned. The priesthood has therefore been changed, and the next verse will adduce still another proof of this.

7:15. The priesthood has been changed, not only in tribe, but in the quality and sort of its priest. This point makes **far more evident** than the former point the change. A priest has arisen now who is **another** in quality and kind. He is a different type of priest, not resembling the Levitical priests at all, but after the likeness of **Melchizedek**.

7:16. Christ has become a priest twice-different in nature from the sons of Aaron. His priesthood rests not on **the law of a carnal commandment** but on **the power of an endless life.** Old Testament priests were priests by virtue of a **law**, outside and apart from themselves or their personal fitness. That law did not attempt to select on the basis of moral or spiritual qualities, but simply according to physical ancestors. It was thus a **carnal commandment**, having to do only with physical restrictions and requirements.

Christ has been made priest, not on this basis, but because He possesses an inherent **power** that fits Him for the position He is to occupy. The term **power** here does not signify authority, but might, and speaks of a characteristic of Christ Himself, inherent in His righteous person. This was the **power** or might of an **endless life.**

Because He was not a sinner, though He was fully tempted, the Son of God could not be held by Satan in death (see comments at 2:14). He possessed the strength or dynamic of a life that, literally, "could not break down." A perfect life has no weak spot; sin is the weakness which brings down all other men, including the Old Testament priests. Christ's priesthood and service are firmly grounded in the inherent power of a life that will never end. The writer will return to this wonderful thought in verse 25.

17 For he testifieth, Thou art a priest for ever after
the order of Melchizedek.

18 For there is verily a disannulling of the commandment going before for the weakness and unprofitableness
thereof.

19 For the law made nothing perfect, but the bringing
in of a better hope did; by the which we draw nigh unto
God.

7:17. To this agrees the Scripture introduced much
earlier (Psalm 110:4) which says, "Thou art a priest for ever
after the order of Melchizedek."

7:18. The familiar Greek construction "on the one
hand/on the other hand" is used in verses 18 and 19. On the
one hand there is a **disannulling** or placing aside or removing
of the previous or former **commandment** regulating priests
(verses 5, 16). This setting aside was necessary because of
the inherent **weakness** and **unprofitableness** of that system
which could not bring perfection (verse 11), which was based
on a carnal requirement (verse 16) and which was manned
by imperfect priests (verses 27-28).

7:19. **The law made nothing perfect** (see Romans 8:3;
Galatians 2:21; 3:21), for it rested on a priesthood which
could not perfect (verse 11). "The law made beginnings,
taught rudiments, gave initial impulses, hinted, foreshadowed, but brought nothing to perfection, did not in itself provide for man's perfect entrance into God's fellowship"
(Expositor's Greek Testament).

Perfection did come, however, in Christ's work and in
the **better hope** which He introduced and confirmed. **Better**
is a key word in Hebrews, and the serious student will profit from a study of its many occurrences in this epistle.
The **hope** spoken of here has already been discussed to some
extent (see notes on 6:18-20).

The blessed feature of this hope, and the ultimate
basis of comparison between all that belonged to the inadequate Old system and all that pertains to the perfect New, is
that by it **we draw nigh unto God.** The verb translated **draw
nigh** is the same one used in the Greek Old Testament at
Exodus 19:21, when, at the giving of the Law, God specifi-

20   And inasmuch as not without an oath he was made
priest:

21   (For those priests were made without an oath; but
this was an oath by him that said unto him, The Lord sware
and will not repent, Thou art a priest for ever after the
order of Melchizedek:)

---

cally commanded the people not to draw near to God. They
could not draw near to God under that system because their
lives were unholy and their sins were ever-present. Under
the covenant of the Son, men in themselves are no better,
but they can draw near to God by virtue of Christ's life
which is holy and His blood which atones for their sins.
Such a blessed thought this is for meditation and such a
holy basis for living!

7:20-22. The three verses go together, joined in the
Greek and English by the connecting phrases translated
inasmuch as (verse 20) and by so much (verse 22), and including verse 21 which is parenthetical. The author presents
a ratio. Inasmuch as, or to the extent, that Christ supercedes
the Old Testament priests by an oath-appointment versus
a simple appointment, by so much or to that same extent,
Jesus is surety of a better testament than theirs.

It was not without an oath that Christ became priest;
rather it was with an oath. This is proved by a chief passage on the subject, Psalm 110:4. Jehovah sware to Jesus,
"Thou art a priest forever after the order of Melchizedek."
Earlier the Hebrews author dealt with the forever in this
psalm; here he is concerned with the sware.

To say that God will not repent does not speak of repentance of sin, for by nature God can not sin. Repent here
is not the word normally translated that way (which itself
has the basic meaning "to change the mind," see 12:17),
but stands for a word which emphasizes the thought of concern or care. God will not change His mind because of
afterthought or later concern, as He did — for example —
with the house of Eli (see I Samuel 2:27-36). Christ is a
priest forever.

Because God will never change His mind about Christ,
Jesus has become surety of a better testament. The word

22 By so much was Jesus made a surety of a better testament.

23 And they truly were many priests, because they were not suffered to continue by reason of death:

24 But this man, because he continueth ever, hath an unchangeable priesthood.

---

translated **surety** is a noun form of the verb translated "draw nigh" in verse 19 (see comments there). The same life of Jesus which enables us to draw nigh to God remains forever, because Jesus has the "power of an endless life" (verse 16). Nor will God change His mind about that life presented as an offering, for He has so given His oath (verse 21). Jesus is therefore **surety** of His covenant. He is a guarantor to man from God that God has accepted a perfect sacrifice on man's behalf. And Jesus ever lives to make intercession for them that come to God by Him (verse 25).

Testament appears here for the first time in Hebrews, and will be discussed in the following chapters. The same word is sometimes translated "covenant," though in the Old and New Testament Scriptures it frequently has the force of a one-sided disposition or will involving two parties, rather than a two-sided agreement or bargain between equals. God's **testament** or covenant is given to man by God; man accepts or rejects it, but he may not change it. More on this later.

7:23. **They** who served under the Old covenant **were many priests,** one taking the place of the other **because** no single one could **continue** in the priesthood forever **by reason of** his own **death.** Josephus says that 83 high priests officiated from Aaron to the destruction of the Temple in A.D. 70. Our writer gives no specific number but notes simply that they all died!

7:24. In contrast to this, Jesus has **an unchangeable priesthood** because He **continueth forever.** He will never die. He will never need a successor. His priesthood is authenticated by God's oath. In short, His is an unerring and immovable priesthood and priestly service. It is perfect in every sense of the word.

25 Wherefore he is able also to save them to the
uttermost that come unto God by him, seeing he ever liveth
to make intercession for them.

7:25. **Wherefore,** because of all these considerations,
Christ is able to save to the uttermost. This may be taken
either with regard to time (He saves forever), or extent
(He saves completely), or both. Neither should be excluded.
Both are true. Christ's complete and eternal salvation is for
them that come to God by him. They are those who come
to Him as priest, who lay their sins on Him as God's Lamb,
who trust His offering of a perfect life as sufficient in God's
sight for blessing, and who by faithful perseverance rely
on His intercession for all these things. It is for no one else,
though "whosoever will" may take advantage of it, and it is
offered by God to all men.

Christ is priest because He has the power of an endless
life. Because **he ever liveth,** He needs no successor. He now
sits beside the Father **to make intercession for** His people.

Christ made but one sacrifice, but He ever lives to make
intercession on the basis of that sacrifice. In terms of His
death, He was the sin-offering. In terms of His resurrection
and present work, He is high priest. The priest of the Old
Testament did not merely kill the sacrifice; he then presented its blood, standing for its life, as an appeal to God for
forgiveness and blessing (Leviticus 17:11-12). In both parti-
culars he had an imperfect priesthood. The sacrifice was
amoral and could not take away sin (see 10:1-4); the priest
was mortal and had to be replaced (as the present chapter
has shown).

Christ, however, offered a perfect sacrifice (His own
sinless life), was then raised (as a sign of God's acceptance
of that life given in death) and will never die again. Unlike
the Old Testament priests and their sacrifices, Christ died
once, but **forever** makes intercession for His people (see I
John 1:7b, 9; 2:1-2).

The one who is in Christ rests his salvation, forgiveness
and hope of blessing on the vicarious death and perfect
obedience of Jesus his high priest. Because Jesus died,
though sinless, He was able to be sin-bearer, "taking away

26 For such an high priest became us, who is holy, harmless, undefiled, separate from sinners, and made higher than the heavens;

27 Who needeth not daily, as those high priests, to offer up sacrifice, first for his own sins, and then for the people's: for this he did once, when he offered up himself.

28 For the law maketh men high priests which have infirmity; but the word of the oath, which was since the law, maketh the Son, who is consecrated for evermore.

---

the sins of the world." Because He offered God a sinless life, the Father is pleased with one Man (though with no other on his own merit) and is justly able to dispense full blessings. Yet because the Christian is one with Christ, His death counts for him and His life does as well. God can, therefore, forgive the one "in Christ" on the basis of Christ's blood and can also give him every blessing and favor on the basis of Christ's life so long as he clings to Him in faith (see Isaiah 53:4-6, 10-12; Romans 4:25; 5:8-11; II Corinthians 5:21; I Peter 2:24; Revelation 1:5; 7:9-17).

7:26. **Such an high priest** as Christ is just what man needs. He **became us,** that is, He was fitted to our needs. Man needs a priest who is **holy,** for he himself is not. The word translated **holy** here also includes the idea of compassion and tender mercy. Man's priest must be **undefiled** and **separate from sinners,** but every Aaronic priest was weak and sinful. Our priest needs to be **higher than the heavens,** living forever to intercede on our behalf.

7:27. Christ does not need **daily** to make a sacrifice **for his own sins** and **then for the people's.** He had no sin Himself, and so He offered **himself** as a perfect sacrifice for the people. Because He had a perfect sacrifice He did not need to offer it but **once.**

7:28. **The law** of the Old Testament priesthood made men high priests who had **infirmity** or weakness. In contrast to this the **word of the oath** (see verse 21), which was **since the law** in origin but replaced it, made the **Son** a priest — and He is **consecrated for evermore.**

The beautiful point of these last verses found wonder-

CHAPTER 8

1 Now of the things which we have spoken this is the sum: We have such an high priest, who is set on the right hand of the throne of the Majesty in the heavens;

---

ful expression in the following hymn, written in 1742 by Charles Wesley.

Arise, my soul, arise, shake off thy guilty fears:
The bleeding Sacrifice in my behalf appears.
Before the Throne my Surety stands;
My name is written on His hands.

He ever lives above, for me to intercede
His all-redeeming love, His precious blood to plead;
His blood atoned for every race,
And sprinkles now the throne of grace.

Five bleeding wounds He bears, received on Calvary.
They pour effectual prayers; they strongly plead for me.
"Forgive him, O forgive," they cry,
"Nor let that ransomed sinner die!"

My God is reconciled; His pard'ning voice I hear;
He owns me for His child; I can no longer fear.
With confidence I now draw nigh,
And "Father, Abba, Father!" cry.

CHAPTER EIGHT

8:1. Of the things spoken in this treatise, **this** which the author is about to say is the **sum** or, as better translated in the later versions, the chief point. And what is this chief point? That we believers have Jesus as **high priest,** and that He is performing priestly service for us at **the right hand** of God **in the heavens.**

This figure of Christ at God's right hand comes from Psalm 110 (see notes at 1:13) and is frequently joined in the New Testament to that of the authoritative "Son of Man" of Daniel, chapter seven. The psalm also combines Christ's priestly and His royal offices. While most other New Testament references to the psalm point to its royal imagery (but see Romans 8:34), the epistle to the Hebrews pays special attention to the priestly.

EXPOSITION 81

2 A minister of the sanctuary, and of the true tabernacle, which the Lord pitched, and not man.

3 For every high priest is ordained to offer gifts and sacrifices: wherefore it is of necessity that this man have somewhat also to offer.

4 For if he were on earth, he should not be a priest, seeing that there are priests that offer gifts according to the law:

8:2. Jesus is a **minister** or, literally, "public servant" of **the sanctuary** or holy things. But His service involves **the true** or substantial **tabernacle which the Lord pitched, not** any structure erected by **man.** His sanctuary is heaven itself, the "most holy place" where God dwells.

While it is true that the physical body of Jesus is referred to as a temple (John 2:19-22), that is not meant here, for verse five says that Moses used this sanctuary for a pattern. Nor does the text speak of the spiritual body of Christ, the church, for the church has the benefit of service performed in this sanctuary; it is not itself the sanctuary. In addition, the "church in the wilderness" corresponds in the present analogy to the New Testament "church" (if we extend the analogy to include either), and each "church" has, not is, its own sanctuary and priestly service.

8:3. Because **every high priest** holds office for the express purpose of offering **gifts and sacrifices** (see note at 5:1), Jesus **of necessity** must also **have** something **to offer,** for He is our high priest. What is true in general is true in particular. Here the emphasis is on the fact of His service; what He offers is told in 7:27.

8:4. This very fact indicates that His ministry is in heaven, not **on earth,** for His sacrifice would not fit the earthly system. Besides, there are no vacancies in the Jewish priesthood for a priest such as He (see also 7:13-14). Christ is our high priest — that has already been established. Yet if His service were earthly, He could not even be a regular priest, much less a high priest (see Numbers 18:1-7). In the Greek, this verse contains the first part of a phrase which is completed in verse six and means "on the one hand . . . on the other hand."

5   Who serve unto the example and shadow of heavenly things, as Moses was admonished of God when he was
about to make the tabernacle: for, See, saith he, that thou
make all things according to the pattern showed to thee
in the mount.

8:5. The earthly priests of the Jewish system do not
serve the substantial, true (verse two) heavenly things,
but rather the example or copy or outline and shadow of
those things. A shadow is not itself the solid reality, but
gives assurance that the substantial object exists of which
it is an outline or copy.

That this Old Testament tabernacle was but a copy of the
heavenly reality and not the original prototype is seen
in the command concerning its erection. Moses was admonished by God in Exodus 25:40 to make all things according to the pattern which he was shown in the mountain.
It is said by some of the rabbis that Gabriel descended
in a workman's apron from heaven with models of the
tabernacle furniture which he showed Moses how to build.
The Bible does not give such details, but simply states that
Moses was shown a pattern (literally something struck from
a die or stamp) and told to build with it as a reference in
all things.

What Moses built, though by God's instruction and according to a divine pattern, was not the original and substantial sanctuary but a copy of it. No man or group of
men can build the true sanctuary, for it is pitched by the
Lord, not by man (verse two; 3:4).

The point here was not altogether new to the Jews,
though the application was. An uninspired Jewish writer
of the period just before Christ had said of Solomon's temple: "Thou gavest command to build a sanctuary in thy
holy mountain, and an altar in the city of thy habitation; a
copy of the holy tabernacle which thou preparedst afore-
hand from the beginning" (Wisdom 9:8). That writer had
surmised that the earthly sanctuaries were copies; it remained for our author to tell the real original and for our
high priest to enter and serve in it!

To have the benefits of a perfect sacrifice administered
by a perfect high priest serving in the true sanctuary built

6 But now hath he obtained a more excellent ministry, by how much also he is the mediator of a better covenant, which was established upon better promises.

7 For if that first covenant had been faultless, then

---

by God and not man is a grace given for the first time to God's covenant people in Christ. We have no mere copy or shadow, but the original holy things of heaven themselves — now fully revealed and fully served by the Son who is Priest-King.

8:6. This verse gives "the other hand" in contrast to the truth stated in verse four. Christ has **now** in this age of fulfillment and reality **obtained a more excellent ministry** or service than that from which He is barred by tribe and nature on earth. To the same extent, He is **mediator** or middle-man of a **better covenant** than that served by the Jewish priests, for His is **established** or legalized on the basis of **better promises** than theirs. The writer enumerates these promises in the rest of the chapter.

The first covenant was also given through a mediator (Galatians 3:19) and the people approached God through him (Exodus 20:19). But while Moses was mediator and Aaron high priest, Jesus is both! In the century before Christ, certain Pharisees looked for a Messiah who would save both Jews and gentiles, and they spoke of a mediator who would intercede before God for the righteous (Testament of Dan 5-6). Yet even these lofty dreams failed to anticipate the plans of God, for we have one who is high priest, mediator and universal Savior combined — and not even from Levi's tribe.

The same may be said with reference to the Qumran Jews described in the Dead Sea Scrolls. They seemed to have looked for two or perhaps three Messiahs; apparently they could not envision one man doing all that needed to be done. But God's Son — higher than any angel — did all that God saw required, and far surpassed the very thoughts and desires of His own people! "How much better," the Hebrews author affirms over and over!

8:7. **If the first** covenant (this word is added by the

should no place have been sought for the second.

8 For finding fault with them, he saith, Behold, the days come, saith the Lord, when I will make a new cove-

---

translators and is therefore in italics) **has been faultless, no place would have been sought** by God or needed by man **for a second** arrangement. Yet God did propose a new covenant, even in the former period of time, and spoke of it then to His people. Therefore, the writer argues, that first was not faultless (see 7:18-19).

8:8. The **fault** lay with the people to whom the first covenant was given, because they did not keep their part of the arrangement. Yet the first covenant was of such nature that all blessings depended on the ability of the people to do just that. This made the covenant itself faulty in effect, or from the point of view of the people. Because of the fault that lay **with them,** God promised a new covenant in Jeremiah 31:31-34, and the author of Hebrews quotes that passage in verses 8-12.

Jeremiah began to prophesy just five years before the great reform of Josiah described in II Kings 23. After centuries of neglect of the Law, the nation affirmed again its commitment to God in a great covenant-renewal ceremony led by the king himself (verses one through three). Only a few years passed, however, until the zeal was dampened and the promises forgotten. Many had never been sincere in their pledge to God's covenant (Jeremiah 3:10) and most of the rest were victims of time and circumstance. The covenant was not in their hearts, and even a royal service could not put it there to stay. Because of this inherent weakness of the people and derived weakness of the covenant, God promised Jeremiah that He would make a new arrangement with His people in the future.

The days come is literally "days are coming." See comments on the "last days" at 1:2. The **new covenant** was promised through Jeremiah 600 years before Christ, but Jesus used the expression in instituting the Lord's Supper (Luke 22:20) and Paul repeated it in the same connection (I Corinthians 11:25). Paul also used the phrase in a ministry context (II Corinthians 3:6). Outside this chapter of He-

enant with the house of Israel and with the house of Judah:

9 Not according to the covenant that I made with
their fathers in the day when I took them by the hand
to lead them out of the land of Egypt; because they con-

---

brews, the term appears only at 9:15 except for these passages.

New here signifies "fresh," not simply new in terms of
time. Hebrews 12:24 uses a different word to call this covenant "new" in time as well. The point of the present word
is that our covenant is fresh and of a different sort from
the old arrangement between God and His people.

The Greek Old Testament, which our writer quotes,
said "covenant a new covenant." He changes that to "perfect
a new covenant," with the same concern for the perfection
or completion of the Christian system as stressed already
in 2:10; 5:9; 6:1; 7:11, 28 and other places.

This fresh new kind of covenant would be made with
the house or people or family of Israel and that of Judah.
In Jeremiah's time the people had been long scattered from
Israel by Assyria, and Judah was even then being carried
captive by Babylon. Yet God would bring back a remnant
from both (Jeremiah 31:7-9) and would establish a new
order.

Jesus was God's fulfillment and fulfiller of all spiritual
promises to the Jews, according to Romans 15:8. Yet the
next ten verses of that chapter show from the Old Testament
that gentiles are also to be beneficiaries of gospel grace. The
book of Hebrews is addressed to Christian Jews, and our
author does not concern himself at this point with the
gentile mission.

8:9. This new kind of covenant will not be like that
one made with the Jews at Sinai, though that one came
from a God whose gracious and powerful acts of deliverance
had brought His people together to receive it. Jeremiah
speaks of God's merciful deliverance in the Exodus in saying
that He took them by the hand to lead them out of the land
of Egypt. The figure is that of a tender father gently leading a small and still-wobbly son before he has learned to care

tinued not in my covenant, and I regarded them not, saith
the Lord.

10   For this is the covenant that I will make with the
house of Israel after those days, saith the Lord; I will put
my laws into their mind, and write them in their hearts:
and I will be to them a God, and they shall be to me a
people:

---

for himself. Such imagery is not uncommon in the Old Testament (Hosea 11:1-3; Deuteronomy 1:31). Similar imagery is
employed of Christ and His new-covenant people at 2:16
(see the comment there).

In spite of God's tender care for Israel, they continued
not in the covenant to fulfill their part of it, and God regarded them not, as a lord whose subjects had failed to keep
what was required of them. Our text of Jeremiah has "although I was a husband to them," which some translate
"and I was as a lord to them," with the sense stated above.
It has also been suggested that a certain Hebrew word for
"disregard" is only one letter different from the Hebrew word
for "husband" or "lord," and that this might explain the difference in readings. In either case the point is the same and
the matter is of little importance for understanding.

8:10. The first of the better promises is given. God's
laws are given in a special people-God relationship under both
the old and new covenants (Exodus 6:7), but here is a difference. Under the former covenant the laws were written
on stone tablets, external to the people. Under the new
covenant the laws are put into their mind and written in
their hearts. Paul makes a similar point in a covenant context at II Corinthians 3:3-18 (see also Romans 8:4; 12:2;
Ephesians 3:16-20; 4:23-24; Philippians 2:12-13; Colossians
3:9-10; I Thessalonians 2:13; II Thessalonians 1:11-12; Hebrews 4:2; James 1:21).

When true regeneration takes place, the Christian finds
God's laws to be in accord with the spirit within him.
Apart from the fleshly nature against which he must continually battle, he will delight in the laws of God and find
them perfectly suited to his own spiritual inclinations. They
are not external and foreign to his nature; he has become
partaker of the divine nature and to that new nature
they are exactly fitted.

11 And they shall not teach every man his neighbor, and every man his brother, saying, Know the Lord: for all shall know me, from the least to the greatest.

12 For I will be merciful to their unrighteousness, and their sins and their iniquities will I remember no more.

8:11. A second promise is that all who are God's people under the new covenant will **know** Him personally. **From the least to the greatest** no individual covered by the new arrangement is excluded. The covenant at Sinai was entered by a nation including many who did not know God personally until after they were involved in the covenant. All who were later born into the relationship as Jews had to be taught of God and learn His former acts of deliverance and provision.

The new covenant is entered by individuals, one by one, and only on the knowledge of God and His saving acts in Christ (see John 6:44-45). Those entering the new covenant already know what God has done for them in the Son. They will to commit themselves to Him in the confidence that His work is sufficient for their pardon and blessing. They signify both their knowledge and their intention by the obedience of faith in baptism.

When one has entered this relationship with God as one among His covenant people, he already knows God as his own saving God. There is no need for those who are in the covenant to be teaching each other a knowledge of God in this sense. Each **brother** and each **neighbor** or fellow-citizen in the new commonwealth already has that knowledge.

8:12. A third promise is given, concerning forgiveness of sins by a merciful God. The people of the first covenant were given laws externally inscribed and foreign to their nature. When they broke those laws, as they always did, no sacrifice could remove the memory of that sin. The people of the fresh and new covenant have God's laws in their hearts and minds (this does not detract from but increases a hunger and thirst for the written Word of God). These laws are compatible with their new nature. When they do

13 In that he saith, A new covenant, he hath made the
first old. Now that which decayeth and waxeth old is ready
to vanish away.

CHAPTER 9

1 Then verily the first covenant had also ordinances
of divine service, and a worldly sanctuary.

---

break them, as they sometimes will, forgiveness is already
available on the basis of the sacrifice of Jesus (see 10:1ff).

8:13. This verse is the author's inspired comment regarding the words spoken by Jeremiah so many centuries
before. In that Jeremiah saith "A new covenant," he (Jeremiah) hath made the first old by contrast — and that was
six centuries before Christ! Our writer is saying concerning
Jeremiah's statement: "By saying 'new,' Jeremiah has long
since antiquated the old."

If it was old in Jeremiah's day (and Jeremiah by implication says that it was), how much older it is when Hebrews
is written! It is, in fact, ready to vanish away, to pass from
view, to completely disappear. Lenski speaks picturesquely
of the old covenant here as "tottering with senility" and
"like an old, old man who is sinking into his grave."

CHAPTER NINE

Our author has spoken already of the legitimacy of
Christ's priesthood (chapter five), which he carefully explained as after the order of Melchizedek (chapter seven).
Because this kind of priest can not serve under the old
covenant, Christ has also mediated a new covenant suitable
to His work (chapter eight). Chaper nine contrasts the
sanctuaries and the rituals of the two covenants, and then,
by a play on words, demonstrates another blessing Christ's
death gives His people.

9:1. The first covenant involved ordinances and arrange-
ments for divine service, but the sanctuary in which these
were carried out was worldly. It was, as verse nine will
show, a figure of something more substantial in the eternal
order.

2 For there was a tabernacle made; the first, wherein was the candlestick, and the table, and the shewbread; which is called the sanctuary.

3 And after the second veil, the tabernacle which is called the Holiest of all;

4 Which had the golden censer, and the ark of the covenant overlaid round about with gold, wherein was the golden pot that had manna, and Aaron's rod that budded,

---

9:2. The Mosaic Tabernacle consisted of two tent-compartments. In **the first** or outer one was **the candlestick** (better, lampstand; Exodus 25:31-40; Leviticus 24:1-4), and **the table** (Exodus 25:23-30; Leviticus 24:6) on which the priests placed the **shewbread** (literally "loaves of presentation" or "bread of the presence"; see Exodus 25:30; Leviticus 24:5-9). This first tent was called the **sanctuary** or holy place.

9:3. A **veil** or curtain (Exodus 26:31-33) separated the holy place from the **holiest of all** or the most holy place (literally, "holy of holies"). It is called the **second** veil in contrast to the linen curtain separating the holy place from the outside court (Exodus 26:36-37).

9:4. The second compartment **had** or involved the use of the **golden censer** or altar of incense (Exodus 30:1-9). Although this altar was in the outer holy place (Exodus 30:6), the smoke from it filled the most holy place on the Day of Atonement so that the high priest never came into God's clear presence (Exodus 30:10; Leviticus 16:12-13).

The **ark of the covenant** was also in the inner tent (Exodus 25:10-15). In connection with this gold-plated wooden chest were three articles which reminded Israel of God's covenant-mercies.

The **golden pot that had manna** (Exodus 16:32-34) reminded Israel of God's miraculous provision of food in the wilderness. The English Bible follows the Hebrew in not mentioning the vessel being gold, but our author is quoting from the Greek version which included that detail.

Aaron's rod that budded (Numbers 17:1-11) was a perpetual sign of the exclusive right of Aaron and his

and the tables of the covenant;

5 And over it the cherubim of glory shadowing the mercy-seat; of which we cannot now speak particularly.

---

descendants to the priesthood. This rod was involved in the miraculous incident which occurred after the rebellion led by Korah (Numbers 16). See also notes on 5:4-6.

The **tables** or plaques **of the covenant** were the two tablets of stone cut by Moses after he had angrily shattered the first tablets because of Israel's idolatry (Exodus 32:19; 34:1-4, 28-29). On these were engraved the ten commandments.

Archaeology has suggested an interesting possibility regarding the dual tablets of stone. In the absence of carbon paper or photocopy machines, covenant-treaties in the ancient world between protective lord and a vassal people were often written twice — one copy for his records and one for theirs. These tablets would be kept in the respective temples as solemn reminders of the covenant. Because Israel's sanctuary was at the same time God's only visible "dwelling," both copies of the "covenant" were kept in the most holy place. Whether the two tablets reflected this practice or not, they gave the ark containing them its name.

When Solomon built the Temple, nothing was in the ark but the two tables of stone (I Kings 8:9; II Chronicles 5:10). The other articles may have been removed during the seven months the Philistines possessed the ark (I Samuel 4: 11; 6:1).

Scripture does not tell the final destiny of the tabernacle or its furniture. An ancient Jewish tradition had Jeremiah taking the tabernacle, the ark and the altar of incense to a cave atop Mount Pisgah, where he hid them "until God shall gather the people again together, and mercy come . . . and the glory of the Lord shall be seen, even the Cloud" (II Maccabees 2:1-8).

9:5. **Over** the ark was a lid of solid gold called **the mercy-seat (Exodus 25:17).** The Greek word here is the same translated "propitiation" in Romans 3:25, where Christ is our mercy-seat. These are the only two times this word appears in the New Testament Scriptures.

6 Now when these things were thus ordained, the priests went always into the first tabernacle, accomplishing the service of God.

7 But into the second went the high priest alone once every year, not without blood, which he offered for himself, and for the errors of the people:

8 The Holy Ghost this signifying, that the way into the holiest of all was not yet made manifest, while as the

---

Connected to the ends of the mercy-seat were the **cherubims of glory,** two golden angels facing each other with upspread wings that covered the mercy-seat (Exodus 25:18-20). From here God would give His commandments (Exodus 25:22) and here He would "meet" the high priest on the Day of Atonement (Leviticus 16:2, 13-15).

Our author speaks only generally of these items which were in the tabernacle. That he **cannot now speak particularly** means simply that he will not at this point enter on a detailed discussion of the individual pieces. Since he makes only a general typological point regarding these items, we will here do the same.

9:6-7. Having spoken of the equipment of the Aaronic priests, he turns now to their ritual. These two verses emphasize one theme in three ways: the inaccessibility of the most holy place under the former covenant. **The priests** ministered in the holy place; **the high priest alone** could enter the most holy place. **Service** was performed **always** or daily in the first tent; it was performed in the second tent only one day **every year.** The outer tabernacle was entered for many purposes; the inner tent could **not** be entered **without blood.** This blood the high priest offered that single day each year, first **for himself** and then for the **errors of the people** (see 5:3; 7:27; Leviticus 16:6, 11, 15).

When these things were thus ordained refers to the time of Moses. The phrase has no bearing on the date of this epistle.

9:8. In the very limited access to the most holy place, the **Holy Ghost** or Spirit was **signifying that the way** to God **was not yet made manifest** to sinful man. So long **as the** first tabernacle was yet standing:

9 Which was a figure for the time then present, in which were offered both gifts and sacrifices, that could not make him that did the service perfect, as pertaining to the conscience;

10 Which stood only in meats and drinks, and divers washings, and carnal ordinances, imposed on them until the time of reformation.

11 But Christ being come an high priest of good things to come, by a greater and more perfect tabernacle,

---

first tabernacle was standing, so long as there were two tents, just that long man could not approach God directly or with a clear conscience. The next chapter will show that the work of Jesus has opened the road to God for the people of the new covenant (10:19-20; see Matthew 27:51; John 10:9; 14:6; Romans 5:2; Ephesians 2:18).

9:9. All this was a figure or parable for the period of time in which the Aaronic priesthood was ministering. It should have indicated to them that their gifts and sacrifices (see 5:1; 8:3) were not for the perfecting of the conscience.

9:10. Such offerings involved ceremonial cleansing from meats or foods and drinks through various washings and carnal ordinances. The ceremonial laws and the rituals pertaining to them were all temporary, and were imposed only until the time or period of sacred history in which God would effect reformation.

Reformation translates a word which means a straightening, and was used in Greek literature of setting a fracture, repairing roads or houses, or even paying debts. The general meaning is "putting right" or "bringing to a satisfactory state." In this verse, the present period of the priestly work of Messiah Jesus is the time when God is putting right sinful man and bringing to a satisfactory state the ordinances foreshadowed by the incomplete shadows and symbols of the old covenant system.

9:11. Christ having arrived (that is literally what he says), so has the time of reformation just mentioned. He is high priest of all the good things which belong to the

not made with hands, that is to say, not of this building;

12 Neither by the blood of goats and calves, but by his own blood he entered in once into the holy place, having obtained eternal redemption for us.

---

order **to come,** that is, the Messianic order of fulfillment. The phrase "to come" is used several times in Hebrews of the still unrealized future (2:5; 13:14), but the entire epistle agrees that this perfect order has now begun in part, and that its power may already be enjoyed (6:5).

Christ's service involves a **greater** and **more perfect tabernacle** or sanctuary. It is **not made with hands** (see 8:2, 5); in fact, it is **not** a part of **this** physical creation or **building.**

9:12. Nor is His service dependent on the **blood of goats** for Himself or of **calves** for the people. Through the merits of the sinless life represented **in his own blood** He has **entered into the** most **holy place once** for all time, and there He has found or **obtained** a **redemption** that is **eternal.**

Unlike the temporary elements of the first covenant, all that pertains to the new covenant belongs to the **eternal** order. This eternal covenant (13:20) brings an eternal redemption (9:12), inheritance (9:15) and salvation (5:9), because it rests on the offering of Christ by His eternal Spirit (9:14).

This is not a Platonic distinction between the world of true being and that of forms or appearance. It is not simply a lower and an upper world. Rather the writer of Hebrews speaks of the eternal things and the carnal ordinances with both horizontal and vertical significance.

On the one hand, there is an eternal realm which exists at the same time as but transcendent to the first-covenant types and shadows based on it. On the other hand, this eternal realm was manifested in the course of human time and history, displacing the former types and shadows.

In combining these concepts the writer is in complete accord with the rest of the New Testament Scriptures that the Christian order involves both what already has come into human history and what has not yet appeared. It is un-

> 13 For if the blood of bulls and of goats, and the
> ashes of an heifer sprinkling the unclean, sanctifieth to the
> purifying of the flesh:
>
> 14 How much more shall the blood of Christ, who
> through the eternal Spirit offered himself without spot to
> God, purge your conscience from dead works to serve the
> living God?

---

fair to our author to say that he is voicing Greek philosophy,
or even that he is speaking in Platonic terms. He is rather
speaking in language that is common to Jewish expression
(the "vertical" typology) on the one hand, and to Christian
teaching (the "horizontal" element) on the other.

9:13. Here is another of those "how much more" contrasts with which we have become familiar in Hebrews.
This time it clinches the point made so far in chapter nine:
Christ as a priest ministers a service which excels that of
the Aaronic priests, and, in keeping with that, He gives far
better benefits.

The blood of bulls and of goats was used in sin-offerings
on the Day of Atonement or at other times, and the ashes of
an unblemished red heifer were used in rites of purification
(Numbers 19:1-22). These things could sanctify so far as
purifying the flesh from ceremonial uncleanness, or even
staying God's wrath against sin momentarily.

9:14. Yet how much more, we are asked, will the blood
of Christ cleanse the conscience, not from uncleanness in-
curred through touching a dead body (Numbers 19:11-16),
but from "practices and attitudes which belong to the way
of death, which pollute the soul and erect a barrier between
it and God" (Bruce) — that is, from dead works?

Freed from such practices by the blood of Christ, His
people are free to serve the living God. Note the contrast
between dead works and a living God. For a similar point
see Romans 6:6, 13; 7:4-6; II Corinthians 2:16; 3:6.

The basis of this superior benefit of Christ's offering
is that He through the eternal spirit offered himself without
spot to God. Christ's sinless life has already been attested
to, and will appear again in chapter ten. His life was "offered" to God, not to Satan as some Medieval theorists sur-

15 And for this cause he is the mediator of the new testament, that by means of death, for the redemption of the transgressions that were under the first testament, they which are called might receive the promise of eternal inheritance.

---

mised. This was a sacrifice of love, but also of "bearing sins." A sinless life could justly meet all God's requirements for man and at the same time pay the ransom for sin. One ought not press these figures beyond scriptural bounds, but simply glory in what God has done and be content to understand that by such terms as He has chosen to use in revealing it.

Through the eternal spirit. In the face of arguments for "spirit" and "Spirit" here, it does no violence to the passage or the larger context to allow both meanings. It was through the offering of His own spirit, first in complete obedience and then in death, that Christ's blood possessed merit. His spirit is eternal because by nature He is the Son who belongs to the eternal order; He was raised to be priest because He possesses an indestructible life (7:16).

On the other hand, it was by anointing Jesus with the Holy Spirit (Isaiah 42:1) that God announced Him to be the Servant on whom He would also lay "the iniquity of us all" (Isaiah 53:6). It was by the Spirit that Christ was raised from the dead (I Peter 3:18) and declared to be the Son (Romans 1:4), fulfilling the promise that He would "prolong His days," "see the travail of His soul and be satisfied" and "justify many" (Isaiah 53:10-11).

9:15. Because of Christ's meritorious blood, by which He became **mediator of the new testament,** one may say that **by means of death** those **who are called** of either covenant **receive the promise of eternal inheritance.** His death was **for the redemption of the transgressions under the first testament,** as well as for sins of those who should live afterward (see also Romans 3:25). Because Christ's blood can cleanse from dead works (verse 14), the **inheritance** contained in God's **promise** is assured to His people.

Having spoken of the **inheritance,** the author's thoughts seem to move for a brief moment to a double meaning possessed by the word which he has been using for "covenant."

16   For where a testament is, there must also of necessity be the death of the testator.

For the word translated "testament" here is the same one translated "covenant" in the preceding chapter.

Because the English language needs two words to express what the Greek language could say in this one, the English reader is at a disadvantage in understanding the present argument until he learns of this double sense.

Ordinarily in Scripture this word means "covenant." It is a great theological word of the Old Testament, where it stands for the Hebrew term signifying the divine disposition or arrangement imposed by God on Israel, through which He brought Israel into a special relationship with Himself. That covenant was one-sided in that God planned and expressed it and Israel could not bargain the terms. But it was two-sided in that Israel accepted certain stated conditions involving both blessing and punishment.

In New Testament times, however, this same Greek word was used commonly for a last will and testament. Not only so, the word for the man who offered a covenant to another was the same word for the man who made a will. There are similarities and differences between these two concepts.

A covenant and a will have in common that both (at least in a divine-human covenant) involve a death. They are distinct inasmuch as such a covenant provides for both benefits and punishments, but a will provides only for benefits — which are assured by the death of the man who makes the will.

In verses 15-20, the word is used both ways. Verses 15, 18-20 use this word in the usual biblical sense of a covenant. But verses 16-17 use the same word (as the Greeks commonly used it) of a will. By this subtle shift in emphasis from one to the other and back again, the author points out a special benefit of the new covenant which the old could not give.

9:16.   **Where a testament** or will **is, there must be** publicly established and proved **the death** of the man who made

17 For a testament is of force after men are dead: otherwise it is of no strength at all while the testator liveth.

---

the will. This is a general statement concerning normal human affairs.

9:17. Such a will is **of force** only after the man who made it is **dead.** It has no legal power while he is living. The point here is not particularly that Jesus was free during His lifetime to dispense blessings in a manner other than that provided for in His "will," though it is true that "the Son of man hath power on earth to forgive sins." Rather the author's concern is that a death must take place in the establishment of either a divine covenant or a human will, and that, in the case of a last will and testament, once the death has occurred the benefits provided by the will are guaranteed to the beneficiaries.

Because the death of Jesus can purge the conscience from dead works, His beneficiaries will receive the eternal inheritance. His new testament is of the nature of a will, as well as that of a covenant (which was discussed in chapter eight), but as a will it provides only benefits!

This does not diminish the force of numerous stern warnings against apostasy. For the beneficiaries of Christ's will are seen to be the people of the new covenant, not individuals in isolation. The benefits are for the "house" which "we" are (3:6). The true rest is for the "people" of God (4:9). Both "house" and "people" figure in the discussion of the new covenant (8:8, 10).

For this reason, individuals are to exhort "one another" lest "any of you" be hardened (3:13). They know that the Lord will judge His "people" (10:30). Some who have entered the covenant may certainly be lost, though only through failure to remain in the covenant by faith (fulness). All who remain among the covenant people will obtain the blessings which Christ's offering secured for them, for His death was that of a testator as well as that of a covenant-mediator. "He is testator and executor in one, surety and mediator alike" (Bruce).

18 Whereupon neither the first testament was dedicated without blood.

19 For when Moses had spoken every precept to all
the people according to the law, he took the blood of calves
and of goats, with water, and scarlet wool, and hyssop, and
sprinkled both the book, and all the people,

20 Saying, This is the blood of the testament which
God hath enjoined unto you.

9:18. Leaving now the idea of a last will and testament,
and returning to the ordinary meaning of covenant, the writer notes that the first covenant or **testament** was also **dedicated** with **blood.**

9:19. **When Moses had spoken** the terms of the covenant
to **all the people,** he sealed with blood their acceptance of
it and God's acceptance of them on that basis. The account
of this covenant-sealing ceremony is given in Exodus 24:1-8.
Several details in Hebrews are not mentioned in the Old
Testament. Exodus makes no mention of goats in the ceremony. It does not mention the use of water, scarlet wool or
hyssop in the sprinkling. It makes no mention of the Book
being sprinkled, but does say the altar was, which Hebrews
omits.

Delitzsch believes the expression "calves and goats" in
Hebrews is a general term for sacrifices of all kinds. It is
also quite possible that our author had information not
given in Exodus.

The mixing of water with blood for sprinkling and
sprinkling by means of wool wrapped around hyssop may
be inferred from the case of the Passover lamb (Exodus
12:22), the purification ceremony for one cleansed of leprosy
(Leviticus 14:4-7, 49-53), or the cleansing of one who had
touched a dead body (Numbers 19:17-18). The author of
Hebrews either assumes the sprinkling of the Book because
the altar and people were sprinkled, or he has information
not extant today.

9:20. Be that as it may, the point he makes is that blood
was directly involved in the dedication of the first covenant,
and he quotes Moses to that effect. He does change the
wording slightly, giving **"this is the blood of the testament"**
for "behold the blood . . ." in Exodus. This may reflect a

21 Moreover he sprinkled with blood both the tabernacle, and all the vessels of the ministry.

22 And almost all things are by the law purged with blood; and without shedding of blood is no remission.

23 It was therefore necessary that the patterns should be purified with these; but the heavenly things themselves

---

simple paraphrase, or he may be aligning those words to the words of institution at the Lord's Supper (Matthew 26:28).

9:21. When the tabernacle was erected, Moses **sprinkled with blood** the **tabernacle** itself and **all the vessels of the ministry.** Again the Old Testament does not give all these details, though it does say the tabernacle and its furnishings were sprinkled with oil (Exodus 40:9-11; Leviticus 8:10-11; Numbers 7:1) and the altar with blood as well (Leviticus 8:15).

Josephus, however, says that the entire tabernacle and furnishings were purified "both with oil first incensed, as I said, and with the blood of bulls and of rams" (Antiquities 3:8:6). Again we may suppose that our author had information beyond that in the books of Moses.

9:22. **Almost all things,** according to the Old Testament **law, were purged with blood.** This statement leaves room for exceptions, as in the case of a poor Israelite (Leviticus 5:11-13; see Numbers 16:46-48; 31:21-24; 31:50-54). The next statement, however, has no exceptions. **Without shedding of blood there is no remission** or forgiveness.

The three words **shedding of blood** stand here for a single Greek word, which is found only here in all biblical literature. This word emphasizes the actual taking of blood, and calls attention to the fact that blood offerings represented the presentation of a life (Leviticus 17:11). Shedding of blood is also linked to the remission of sins in the Lord's words at the Last Supper (Matthew 26:28).

9:23. Because of the general practice of cleansing with blood, and because forgiveness of sins may be obtained only through blood-shedding, **it was necessary** that the **patterns of things in the heavens** (see 8:1, 5) **be purified** with the blood ceremonies already described. But the same principles require that **the heavenly things themselves be purified** with better sacrifices than these.

24 For Christ is not entered into the holy places made with hands, which are the figures of the true; but into heaven itself, now to appear in the presence of God for us:

---

with better sacrifices than these. The heavenly realities are purified with the blood of Christ, and this purification is necessary because of the general curse of sin on creation and because Christ has opened the way for redeemed sinners to enter the most holy place not made with hands.

9:24. **Christ** has **entered** into a holy place **not made with hands** (see 8:1, 2, 5; 9:11-12), not the mere **figures of the true,** but **into heaven itself.** He has gone to **appear in the presence of God,** to be examined as a sacrificial offering, as a Lamb without spot or blemish, to be carefully scrutinized by God Himself — and that with no cloud of incense to obscure the view! Not only so, He has presented Himself in this manner **for us,** and it is for His people alone, not for Himself, that Christ became the Lamb of God or that He made this appearance.

Philip the Evangelist preached Jesus as a lamb, based on a prophetic passage full of the Gospel (Acts 8:32). Peter wrote of the Christian's redemption by the blood of Christ "as of a lamb without blemish" (I Peter 1:19). John the Baptist introduced Jesus as the "Lamb of God that taketh away the sins of the world" (John 1:29, 36). Paul speaks of Christ as our "Passover" (Lamb) who has been slain (I Corinthians 5:7).

The figure of Jesus as a sacrificial lamb appears only in Revelation otherwise, though there frequently. He is the Lamb whose sacrifice has been received; He is a Lamb worthy of praise; the Lamb who has redeemed His people; the Lamb at God's right hand; the Lamb who will come in judgment; and the Lamb who will be forever a light for His people (Revelation 5:6, 8, 12, 13; 6:16; 7:9-17; 12:11; 13:8; 14:1, 4, 10; 15:3; 17:14; 19:7, 9; 21:9, 14, 22, 23, 27; 22:1, 3).

9:25. Because of the quality of His offering, Christ made but one for all time, though as eternal priest He perpetually mediates on the basis of that single sacrifice. Here the contrast is with the Aaronic priesthood. The regular priests

25 Nor yet that he should offer himself often, as the
high priest entereth into the holy place every year with
blood of others;

26 For then must he often have suffered since the
foundation of the world: but now once in the end of the
world hath he appeared to put away sin by the sacrifice of
himself.

---

under that covenant entered the holy place often; the high
priest entered the most holy place one day each year. But
Christ, the priest of the new covenant, entered the heavenly
holy place only one time forever. He does not need to offer
himself often, not even every year, for He did not carry the
blood of others but His own.

9:26. If Christ's single sacrifice were not sufficient for
all time, He must have suffered a bloody death since the
foundation of the world, for just that long men have been
sinners and in need of a sacrifice. But instead we see Him
now in the end of the world, at the consummation of the
ages, when the eternal order is breaking in on man's history,
at the time of perfection — appearing once on the scene of
history to make His single offering and put away or disannul
the power (same word at 7:18) of sin for all time.

Note the contrasts in this verse. Christ has not suffered
death often, but once; not from the foundation of the world,
but only now in the end of the ages; not (as the high priests
of verse 25) with the blood of others, but by the sacrifice
of Himself.

The exact expression here translated the end of the
world (literally, "the consummation of the ages") appears
only here in the New Testament Scriptures. It is parallel,
however, to the expression found at Matthew 13:39, 40, 49;
24:3 and 28:20, and closely related in meaning to similar
phrases in I Corinthians 10:11 and I Peter 1:20. As Bruce
points out, "it is not that Christ happened to come at the
time of fulfillment, but that His coming made that time the
time of fulfillment." See notes on 9:10-12 and especially on
1:2.

The singularity of Christ's offering is expressed here in
three ways. It is once for all; it is in the consummation of

> 27 And as it is appointed unto men once to die, but after this the judgment:
>
> 28 So Christ was once offered to bear the sins of many; and unto them that look for him shall he appear the second time without sin unto salvation.

---

the ages; it is to abolish sin. If sin is abolished, there is no need for another sacrifice. If the consummation of the ages has come, there is no time for another. If Christ's offering is once for all, there can be no other. Chapter ten will show how this once-for-all character of His offering brings both marvelous blessings and a dreadful warning to the people of the new covenant.

9:27. The general rule is stated that **it is appointed** by God **for men to die once** and only once, inasmuch as they live once in a mortal body, and **after this** comes **the judgment**. The author does not deal with the time lapse between death and judgment; that is not his concern. He simply calls attention to the fact that men live one time, die one time and (sometime thereafter) are judged by God for the life they lived before they died.

9:28. In keeping with this general rule, **Christ** (who became one with His human brethren by taking on flesh and blood, 2:14) also lived one time in the flesh, died one time in the flesh and appeared before God one time to be judged on the basis of the single life lived before He died.

Christ, however, lived a representative life on behalf of others (as chapter ten will explain); He died **to bear the sins of many,** so **was offered;** and has been judged for others as well (verse 24). Yet the point remains the same as with all men: He can only live once, die once, and be judged once for that life. But Christ has already lived, died, and been judged — therefore He can not repeat His fleshly life, or death, or (this is the point in relation to verses 25-26) offering.

Not only was Christ's life unique (both because it was sinless and because it was lived for others), and His death one of a kind (because it was offered as a sacrifice, for others, and by Himself), but His "judgment" was the first among men, signifying the beginning of the end of the

CHAPTER 10

1 For the law having a shadow of good things to come, and not the very image of the things, can never with

---

world and guaranteeing the outcome of the judgment of all His people.

The second point in this verse uses imagery of the Day of Atonement. Christ our high priest has entered the presence of God bearing the offering. His people, meanwhile, are waiting outside the sanctuary for Him to return and certify that the sacrifice has been received and that they are forgiven. The Day of Atonement, according to an ancient Jewish source, came to a happy end with the high priest going to his own house. "All the people accompany him . . . and he holds a festival to celebrate his having come successfully out of the sanctuary." See Appendix V.

The writer seems to be saying that our high priest of the new covenant has entered the presence of God with a suitable sin offering, and that He will certainly **appear the second time** to His people **that look for him.** Unlike those priests who foreshadowed and symbolized Him, Christ does not repeat the performance. Having **once** been offered **to bear sins,** He will reappear only to bring **salvation** to those for whom He once suffered. One should not stretch the analogy beyond measure, but we might observe in the light of the rest of the New Testament Scriptures that the Holy Spirit's descent, which authorized the beginning of the preaching of the Gospel, was a case of the high priest sending a messenger out in advance of Himself to tell the waiting people that His sacrifice had been received and that remission of sins was effected.

CHAPTER TEN

10:1. **The law,** standing here for the entire Old Testament economy, offered only a **shadow** of the **good things** which were **to come** in the Messianic era of fulfillment, an era which, with Christ, has already begun (see note at 9:11). It did not minister **the very image** of heavenly realities but mere types and shadows. The thought here is the **same as** at

those sacrifices which they offered year by year continually make the comers thereunto perfect.

2 For then would they not have ceased to be offered? because that the worshippers once purged should have had no more conscience of sins.

3 But in those sacrifices there is a remembrance again made of sins every year.

4 For it is not possible that the blood of bulls and of goats should take away sins.

8:2, 5; 9:1, although the words used are different.

Since perfection belongs to the new order and not to the former, it is not surprising that worshippers under the old were not made **perfect**. That they were not is evident in the offering of **the same sacrifices** one **year** after another, **continually.**

10:2. If the **worshippers** had been **purged** or cleansed by those offerings, they would have had no longer a bad **conscience** regarding sins. By contrast see John 13:10; Acts 15:9; I Corinthians 6:11; Hebrews 9:14; I Peter 3:21.

10:3. The opposite was true, however. The offering of jealousy, for example, was "an offering of memorial, bringing iniquity to remembrance" (Numbers 5:15). Even the sacrifices of the Day of Atonement were reminders of past sins (Leviticus 16:21); furthermore, yearly repetition testified to their inability to cover future sins.

A contrast may be noted here between the sacrifices of the old covenant and the Lord's Supper of the new. The former memorialized the sinfulness of the worshippers and constantly reminded them of their shortcomings. The latter memorializes the single sacrifice of Christ, by which worshippers now are constantly cleansed of sin. **Remembrance** here is the same word found in I Corinthians 11:24-25 and may be translated "memorial."

10:4. All that has been said in the first three verses leads to one conclusion: the **blood** of animals can not **take away** the memory of or bad conscience resulting from **sins.**

5 Wherefore when he cometh into the world, he saith,
Sacrifice and offering thou wouldest not, but a body hast
thou prepared me:

6 In burnt offerings and sacrifices for sin thou hast
had no pleasure.

10:5. Foreseeing that animal blood could not take away
sin, God had from eternity planned another offering to
which burnt sacrifices always pointed. What follows must
be seen in the light of this **wherefore**, as the writer begins
to explain the significance of sacrificial **blood** and the forgiveness Christ makes possible.

The purpose of Christ's advent into the **world** as a
man may be expressed in words taken from Psalm 40:6-8,
which our author here puts in His mouth. "**Sacrifice and
offering** of animals or produce is not what You really desire,"
Jesus says to the Father. "You have **prepared** a human
body for **me** instead."

Our author is quoting the Greek Old Testament which
says "a body you have prepared." The Hebrew text says,
"you have dug out my ears." The final meaning is the same,
however, and may be explained along either of two lines.
Ears may stand here for the entire body, the part for the
whole. If God formed ears for the man, He prepared also the
rest of his body.

Approaching the text another way, one may interpret
Christ (or David, originally) to be saying, "You have made
ears that I may hear Your will and do it" (see Isaiah 50:
4-5). Either way the point is the same. God does not desire
a mere multiplication of Old Testament sacrifices and offerings. What He does want from man is indicated by the
gift of a human body. He wants a human life lived according
to His will.

10:6. God has never desired sacrifices above human
obedience. If man had obeyed, in fact, he would not have
needed sacrifices at all. This was true from the beginning
of Israel's history (Jeremiah 7:21-23; I Samuel 15:22; Psalm
51:16-17) to the time of the great writing prophets of the
eighth century (Isaiah 1:11-17; Amos 5:22-24; Micah 6:6-8).

Each type of offering under the old covenant served a
particular purpose, and all are included under the present

7 Then said I, Lo, I come (in the volume of the book it is written of me,) to do thy will, O God.

8 Above when he said, Sacrifice and offering, and burnt offerings and offering for sin thou wouldest not, neither hadst pleasure therein; which are offered by the law;

9 Then said he, Lo, I come to do thy will, O God. He taketh away the first, that he may establish the second.

---

principles. **Sacrifice** was the regular term for the peace-offering, a conciliation for the restoring of fellowship. **Offering** was the generic term for the meal or cereal offering, a donation representing the consecration of the giver. **Burnt offering** indicates the oblation expressing worship. The **sin-offering** was made for expiation or atonement.

Whatever the purpose and whatever the offering, none was God's first choice from man. It is better to maintain fellowship than to restore it, to show consecration by a life than by an offering, to worship by giving oneself than a burnt animal, to obey than to atone for disobedience. God simply wanted human conformity to His will, manifested in sincere and loving obedience. Christ came to give this — and the Father gave Him a body for that purpose.

10:7. The psalm quotation continues. **"I come,"** Jesus says, **"to do thy will, O God."** The parenthetical phrase, **"in the volume of the book it is written of me,"** is also from the psalm. Again, two meanings are possible. Christ may be saying, "what is written in the Law I apply to myself to keep." Or He may mean, "what David said in the psalm regarding obedience was a prophetic statement of Myself and My work." Both are true and both should be included in our understanding.

Psalm 40:8 adds a phrase not quoted here: "Thy law is within my heart." David of old applied what the Law said to his own life, so that God's precepts were not written in the book alone but also inscribed in his heart. How fitting for the Christ to be foretold in such a context! For the new covenant He mediated is characterized by laws inscribed in men's hearts (see 8:10).

10:8-9. Our author comments on the sense of the psalm. Christ first mentioned sacrifices and offerings, he notes, **then**

10 By the which will we are sanctified through the offering of the body of Jesus Christ once for all.

11 And every priest standeth daily ministering and offering oftentimes the same sacrifices, which can never take away sins:

12 But this man, after he had offered one sacrifice for sins for ever, sat down on the right hand of God;

He spoke of His own coming **to do** God's **will.** Christ took away the **first** — the offering of all those sacrifices, to make the **second** stand — human obedience to all God's expressed will for man.

10:10. Because Jesus gave God human obedience in **a** human body, then offered that body in death, **we** who are His people **are sanctified** or made holy on the basis of God's **will** which Jesus perfectly demonstrated in His body. **Will** here is the same as in verses seven and nine; it is not the same word used for a testament-will.

Sanctified here is in a participle form meaning something now the case because of what happened previously. We are those who have been sanctified and still are — because of the past offering of the body (symbolizing the well-pleasing life) of Jesus.

Once for all is emphatic in the original here because of its location in the sentence. We have seen this word already at 7:27 and 9:12. A slightly less intensive form appears at 6:4; 9:7, 26-28; 10:2 and 12:26-27.

10:11. The old testament **priest** performed imperfect service, and stood day after day to repeat often and regularly the same sacrifices; sacrifices which, ironically but logically, could never fully remove sins.

10:12. Jesus, on the other hand, presented **one sacrifice for sins,** His body (or, in other places, His blood), standing for His perfect human life. This was sufficient **for ever.** His offering completed, Jesus has now **sat down.** Delitzsch expresses the contrast of these verses well. "The priest of the Old Testament stands timid and uneasy in the holy place, anxiously performing his awful service there, and hastening to depart when the service is done, as from a place

13 From henceforth expecting till his enemies be made his footstool.

14 For by one offering he hath perfected for ever them that are sanctified.

15 Whereof the Holy Ghost. also is a witness to us: for after that he had said before,

---

where he has no free access, and can never feel at home; whereas Christ sits down in everlasting rest and blessedness at the right hand of Majesty in the holy of holies, His work accomplished, and He awaiting its reward."

The figure of Christ at God's **right hand** is taken from Psalm 110, which our author has used many times. Here he has come almost full cycle from 1:3, and is about to tie up his argument.

10:13-14. Christ as priest has made His offering. Christ as king is waiting for the total subjection of all His subjects. God has made Him king already; Christ now possesses all authority (Matthew 28:18; Ephesians 1:21-22; I Peter 3:22). But not all men have yet acknowledged His authority, though some day they must (I Corinthians 15:24-25; Philippians 2:8-11).

Psalm 110 forms a backdrop before which the risen Christ is seen throughout the New Testament Scriptures. As noted already, most references to the psalm outside Hebrews emphasize Christ's kingship. Hebrews usually stresses His priesthood. Here the two are combined. As priest, Christ has made His offering and His people are waiting for His return. As king, He is at God's right hand, waiting for full recognition by men. As throughout the New Testament writings, the end has already begun but it is not yet completed. We live in the interim.

10:15-17. Those trusting in the sacrifice of Jesus are perpetually and completely sanctified. This has been argued already, and to this the Holy Spirit agrees as witnessed in the Old Testament Scriptures. Our author refers again to Jeremiah 31, which he discussed at length in chapter eight.

16 This is the covenant that I will make with them after those days, saith the Lord, I will put my laws into their hearts, and in their minds will I write them;

17 And their sins and iniquities will I remember no more.

18 Now where remission of these is, there is no more offering for sin.

19 Having therefore, brethren, boldness to enter into the holiest by the blood of Jesus,

---

The Spirit there stated first, "This is the covenant I will make," speaking of Christ's covenant in which laws would be placed in men's hearts and minds. But the Spirit added (our author points out), "and their sins and iniquities will I remember no more."

10:18. Remission of sins means that God does not remember them any longer. Where there is such remission, no more offering is needed for sin. With this, the argument of Hebrews ends. The rest of the epistle consists of exhortations or warnings based on the points already established.

We have a high priest who has offered a perfect offering because it represented a human life perfectly in accord with God's will for man. By that sacrifice, we are perfected. God has promised not to remember our sins any more. There will be no further offering; there is no need for another.

Christ now is mediating the blessed benefits of His once-for-all sacrifice for all His covenant people. He waits for His kingship to be fully recognized. His people wait for His return with the inheritance already secured. The writer of Hebrews urges his readers to be among the faithful who will receive the blessing.

10:19. Boldness here represents a word which has the root idea of freedom of speech, therefore, freedom from fear or inhibition. The phrase, to enter the holiest, may also be translated "boldness for an entrance into the holiest." Both the personal act and the general fact depend on the blood of Jesus.

20 By a new and living way, which he hath consecrated for us, through the veil, that is to say, his flesh;

21 And having an high priest over the house of God;

22 Let us draw near with a true heart in full assurance of faith, having our hearts sprinkled from an evil con-

---

10:20. Our entrance (see Ephesians 3:12) is by means
of a way or road that is new, a particular Greek word which
originally meant "freshly-slain." It is also living, therefore
effectual to attain its desired and intended goal.

Some commentators and translators think his flesh explains the veil, others that it refers to the way. If the former
is intended, the human body of Jesus is a veil separating
His perfect life from God in heaven. His spirit passed
through that flesh on its way to glory. If the latter is meant,
the human body of Jesus is itself the way which He consecrated through the figurative veil separating man from
God. His people travel down the road of His human life
into God's presence. In fact, Jesus did pass through the
flesh to His present position of glory and man must pass
through His human life (that is, the merits it secured) to
find salvation.

In either case, Christ has consecrated or dedicated or
officially opened a new highway from man to God by His
blood. We have confidence to venture upon it because Jesus
has travelled it ahead of us and is now safely in heaven at
God's right hand (see comments at 6:19-20).

10:21. The Christian has also a high priest over the
house of God (see notes at 3:1-6). Having both boldness
and such a high priest, saints are exhorted regarding rela-
tionships with God, their own faith and one another.

10:22. Let Christ's people draw near (the same word in
4:16; 7:25 and 11:6) to the Father with a true heart, a heart
that is sincere and without guile (see the same point in
John 4:23-24). Such an approach is to be in full assurance
of faith, that is, in the complete confidence and total persuasion which faith can give.

We have been separated from dead works by the figurative sprinkling of the blood of Jesus (see 9:13-14); we have

science, and our bodies washed with pure water.

---

been set apart for service to God as well. The priests were
to wash in water before entering the tabernacle to serve
(Leviticus 16:4) — this may be in the mind of the author
here.

I believe that the **hearts sprinkled from an evil conscience** represents the spiritual cleansing of the conscience
by the Holy Spirit, through the merit of the life of Jesus as
represented spiritually by His blood — in other words, the
inner part of regeneration. The **bodies washed with pure
water** represents the physical act of baptism in water, the
divinely-ordained manner by which faith reaches out to
take hold of sovereign grace. It is the **outer** element in regeneration.

It is not uncommon for New Testament writers to speak
of the physical and spiritual together in this way. Jesus
talked of a birth of water and the Spirit (John 3:3, 5). Peter
told his Pentecost audience to be baptized for remission
of sins and the reception of the Holy Spirit (Acts 2:38). Saul
of Tarsus was told to be baptized and wash away his sins,
calling on the name of the Lord (Acts 22:16); neither he
nor Ananias had any doubt that his sins were washed away
by a spiritual cleansing based on the blood of Christ.

We read of the Corinthians being baptized by the Spirit
into one body (I Corinthians 12:13); of the washing of water
by the word (Ephesians 5:26); of merciful salvation by the
washing of regeneration and renewing of the Holy Spirit
(Titus 3:5). Peter makes it clear that baptism is related to
salvation because it is the appeal to God for a good conscience (I Peter 3:21). His careful explanation that baptism
is not merely the removal of bodily defilement shows that
the inner and outer go together and that they might be misunderstood. The same verse emphasizes that baptism saves
"by the resurrection of Jesus Christ."

The **full assurance of faith** is possible just because our
standing is grounded in the finished work and the single offering of Jesus Christ. John Bunyan speaks of God addressing the sinner in these words: "Sinner, thou thinkest that
because of thy sins and infirmities I cannot save thy soul,

23 Let us hold fast the profession of our faith without wavering; (for he is faithful that promised;)

24 And let us consider one another to provoke unto love and to good works:

25 Not forsaking the assembling of ourselves together, as the manner of some is; but exhorting one another: and

---

but behold my Son is by me, and upon Him I look, and not on thee, and will deal with thee according as I am pleased with Him." We are accepted in the Beloved — first, last and always (Ephesians 1:6, KJV); but, praise God, in the Beloved we are accepted!

10:23. Again the exhortation to **hold fast** our own **profession** or commitment **of faith.** The better manuscripts here have "hope," in keeping with previous exhortations (see 3:6, 14; 4:14; 6:11). **God** is the one **that promised,** and God **is faithful,** reliable and trustworthy. No one who commits himself to God in hope will ever be disappointed or betrayed (see also 6:11-12, 18).

10:24. Christ's people must also **consider** or pay attention to **one another,** with an intention **to provoke** or stir up **to love and good works.** The word here translated **provoke** gives the English word "paroxysm," and appears in the New Testament Scriptures only here and at Acts 15:39. The mutual consideration enjoined is the duty of every Christian and is a clear, though frequently neglected, obligation.

10:25. Such holy provocation can not occur with the **forsaking the assembling of ourselves together,** although **some** had done just that. It happens rather by **exhorting** each other in assemblies called for that purpose, as well in the normal course of daily life.

It has been suggested that these readers were still meeting in Jewish synagogue assemblies, but remaining for Christian devotions on the Lord's Day. Some were neglecting this additional assemblying, for which they are chided. Others have suggested that **some** were absenting themselves from the regular assemblies of the saints through pride or party-spirit and were holding private meetings instead.

It is best to take the passage in its context and simply

so much the more, as ye see the day approaching.

---

say that those who have access to God's presence and who
have a high priest in heaven are to draw near to God, hold
fast their own hope, and encourage Christian loving and
living in one another. They will not do this by calling an end
to Christian assemblies (through fear of persecution or simple indifference), but rather by meeting together for exhortation.

Such encouragement is to intensify **as the day** is seen
approaching. Throughout the Old Testament literature "the
day" means an occasion when God visits a people to punish
sin and deliver the righteous. The New Testament writers
also speak of such a final day of punishment and salvation.
Before the destruction of Jerusalem, many early Christians
did not know to separate the end of the Jewish state and
religion from the close of the present age and end of the
world (see Matthew 24:3; Acts 1:6-8). Jesus had taught,
however, that the two would not come together (Matthew
24:33, 36; Mark 13:29, 32).

The author to the Hebrews may write before or after
the climactic days of the closing sixties. Whatever the date,
he speaks of the final **day** of the Lord — the denouement
of all human history at the consummation of the age. His
readers had not learned to separate that "day" into the
separate events of resurrection, judgment and so forth, but
thought of the entire event in terms of the phrase from the
Old Testament.

As Delitzsch puts it, this is "the day of days, the final,
the decisive day of time, the commencing day of eternity,
breaking through and breaking up for the church of the
redeemed the night of the present." It is a poor argument
that believers could not **see** this **day approaching.** James
could urge patience in affliction "for the coming of the Lord
draweth nigh" (5:6-8). Paul could speak of saints "knowing
the time" that "the day is at hand" (Romans 13:11-12). Peter
could write of impending judgment and "the end of all
things" as "at hand" (I Peter 4:5, 7). The word in all three
passages is the word translated **approaching** here. Furthermore, all three contexts contain ethical instruction regarding

26 For if we sin willfully after that we have received the knowledge of the truth, there remaineth no more sacrifice for sins,

27 But a certain fearful looking for of judgment and fiery indignation, which shall devour the adversaries.

---

proper conduct and mutual concern among Christian believers in view of the impending end.

10:26. Warning follows exhortation. To **sin willfully** is not to commit a single sinful act of weakness or ignorance, but, as the Greek verb form indicates, to continue in a constant practice of sin. Nor is **sin** here just any kind of sin, but specifically the sin of disbelief which shows itself in forsaking Christ altogether. While such apostasy may occur gradually (see the warnings of 2:1-3; 6:11-12), it ultimately comes about through an act of the will which rejects Christ and His offering for sin. One might observe that even the Old Testament sacrifices made provision only for sins committed in ignorance or weakness — not for presumptuous or willful sins (Numbers 15:22-31).

What is envisioned here is a rejection of the new covenant, after it has been received with faith and joy. Here is a will to sin in spite of a full **knowledge of the truth**, knowledge being a thorough knowledge both in mind and by personal relationship.

Apostasy from Christ is dreadfully severe because there is **no more sacrifice for sins**. His offering, once for all, is man's last chance and only hope. The person who rejects that — especially the man who has known it personally and then rejected it — is hopelessly lost, for he has set his will against the only basis of forgiveness and the only sacrifice God will accept. Regular assemblying of saints for mutual exhortation is so important because it helps prevent the damnation that comes through loss of faith.

10:27. The deserter may look forward only to **judgment** and **fiery indignation** (see Deuteronomy 9:3; Psalm 79:5; Isaiah 26:11; 30:27; 64:2; Zephaniah 1:18), which is all the more **fearful** because it is **certain**. This judgment is designed for God's **adversaries** or enemies or opponents. One places

28 He that despised Moses' law died without mercy under two or three witnesses:

29 Of how much sorer punishment, suppose ye, shall he be thought worthy, who hath trodden under foot the Son of God, and hath counted the blood of the covenant, wherewith he was sanctified, an unholy thing, and hath done despite unto the Spirit of grace?

---

himself in that category when he forsakes Christ and rejects His sacrifice.

10:28. Under the **law** of **Moses** the man who forsook God's covenant and worshipped idols was stoned to death **without mercy** upon conviction through the testimony of **two or three witnesses** (see Deuteronomy 17:2-7).

10:29. If apostasy under the inferior covenant was hastily and rigidly punished, **how much sorer punishment** must be proper for the man who rejects the new covenant instituted by the blood of the Son of God? The question is left open for consideration by each reader — **suppose ye?**

Rejection of Christ and His offering involves a turning from the most holy elements of divine religion, and that in the cruelest manner. It is to renounce and tread **under foot** (see the same word at Matthew 5:13; 7:6; Luke 8:5) **the Son of God.** It is to regard **the blood of the covenant** (see comments at 9:18-20) which makes man holy **(wherewith he was sanctified)** as itself common and **unholy.** It is to despise the very Spirit of grace.

Do despite translates a word which comes into our language in the noun "hubris." This word was used by the ancient Greeks for the most presumptuous arrogance and haughtiness, and was regarded as the worst possible sin. The idea is seen in various forms of the word translated "entreat spitefully" (Luke 18:32; Matthew 22:6), "use despitefully" (Acts 14:5), "reproach" (II Corinthians 12:10) or "shamefully entreat" (I Thessalonians 2:2). Just as it is cruelly ironic for the covenant blood which makes holy to be regarded as itself unholy, so it is for the **Spirit** whose ministry brings divine **grace** to be rejected with arrogance and insolence!

10:30. We can appreciate the severity of punishment

30 For we know him that hath said, Vengeance belongeth unto me, I will recompense, saith the Lord. And again, The Lord shall judge his people.

31 It is a fearful thing to fall into the hands of the living God.

32 But call to remembrance the former days, in which, after ye were illuminated, ye endured a great fight of afflictions;

---

awaiting such a one, for **we know** God who has claimed **vengeance** as His own prerogative and has promised to **recompense**. These words are probably taken from the Song of Moses (Deuteronomy 32:35), and they are quoted by Paul in urging Christians not to avenge themselves (Romans 12:19).

Another quotation from the Song of Moses shows the severity of divine judgment: **The Lord will judge his people** (Deuteronomy 32:36). This phrase may be interpreted two ways. In the Old Testament passage (see also Psalm 135:14) God judges His people by rescuing them and punishing their enemies. The author of Hebrews may be saying that God will vindicate those who are faithful to Christ in spite of adversity and temptation by punishing those who once knew Him but turned away. Or he may use the term in a general sense to mean that God will condemn the apostates and so "judge" them.

10:31. In either event, the point is the same: **It is a fearful thing to fall into the hands of the living God!** It is **fearful** because He is God, and all-powerful; it is more fearful because He is the **living** God and eternal in wrath.

It is well that we should realize that the Gospel of Jesus Christ is not soft, shallow, or flabby. It **is** a matter of blood and fire, a solemn, and, at times, almost a fierce thing (Robinson).

10:32. Fear of punishment is a powerful incentive; so is the precious memory of early faithfulness. **Call** those **former days** to your mind, he urges. After becoming Christians, or being **illuminated** (see comment at 6:4 where the same word is used), they had **endured** much for their faith.

Great fight here translates a word for an athletic contest — the figure will reappear in 12:1-2. **Afflictions** are

33 Partly, whilst ye were made a gazingstock both by reproaches and afflictions; and partly, whilst ye became companions of them that were so used.

34 For ye had compassion of me in my bonds, and took joyfully the spoiling of your goods, knowing in yourselves that ye have in heaven a better and an enduring substance.

35 Cast not away therefore your confidence, which hath great recompense of reward.

---

literally "pressures" on the Christian. This pressure results from tension, created by the opposing pulls of old nature and new, God and Satan, of the Present Age and the Coming Age.

10:33. On the one hand, our author's first readers had been personally made a gazingstock. This word means to be brought shamefully before public view, as in a theater, and reminds us of the later martyrdom of Christians by wild animals in public displays. These saints had not faced lions or leopards but the spiritual beasts of reproaches (see 11:26; 13:13) and afflictions from their associates.

On the other hand, they had become companions or partners or sharers with other Christians so mistreated for Christ's sake. Used here signifies a way of life characterized by affliction. This is not a one-time occurrence. Under such perpetual and constant attack, the man of faith shows the genuineness of his commitment. This will be the subject of a strong exhortation in the next chapter.

10:34. The Hebrew Christians had shown compassion or sympathy toward those who were imprisoned for their faith. The better manuscripts and later versions have "those in bonds" instead of "me in my bonds." They had experienced the spoiling or snatching away of their own goods or substance, and that with joy. They knew that they had better possessions in heaven, possessions that were enduring, and for those they could endure the plunder of earthly goods.

10:35. They had been faithful before; they can now remain true to Christ. Do not cast away your confidence (see comment at 10:19; see 3:6; 4:16 "boldly"), he urges. It has great wages or recompense of reward (2:2; 11:26).

36 For ye have need of patience, that, after ye have
done the will of God, ye might receive the promise.

37 For yet a little while, and he that shall come will
come, and will not tarry.

38 Now the just shall live by faith: but if any man
draw back, my soul shall have no pleasure in him.

39 But we are not of them who draw back unto perdition; but of them that believe to the saving of the soul.

10:36. Patience means endurance, and is a key note in
the author's song of encouragement. What God has promised
He will surely give (9:15; 11:13, 39-40), but only after faithful endurance according to the **will of God**.

10:37. **Yet a little while,** he urges, taking words from
Isaiah 26:20. The Greek here literally says, "a little — how
very, very little!" By comparison with the ages of eternity,
how very, very well this describes the short Christian conflict on earth! For the same point from the perspective of
saints already martyred, see Revelation 6:9-11.

He that cometh here refers to Christ the high priest.
The author takes the phrase from Habakkuk 2:3 (Greek
version). Christ was "He that Cometh" when He came into
the world as Messiah (see Matthew 11:3; Luke 7:19; John
6:14). He is "He that Cometh" now to the Christian who
awaits His return (see 9:28). Assurance is given that **He will
come** and **will not tarry.** (Prof. Homer Hailey refers this
phrase to the Romans coming against Jerusalem, just as
Habakkuk spoke of Babylonian invaders. This view would
require an early date for Hebrews.)

10:38. Two categories of men are named. **The just** or
righteous will **live** through their **faith** — again words from
Habakkuk (2:4; see also Romans 1:17; Galatians 3:11).
Faith here stresses the element of endurance — with almost
the sense of "hope" in other New Testament epistles. The
second category consists of those who **draw back** in disbelief,
and in them God finds **no pleasure.**

10:39. The exhortation closes with a word of optimism.
We includes the author and his first readers. We are not of
that class who **draw back,** and end in **perdition** or destruction, but of those who **believe** and keep on believing **to the**
resultant **saving of the soul.** The next chapter will demonstrate the character and behavior of saving faith through

CHAPTER 11

1 Now faith is the substance of things hoped for, the evidence of things not seen.

---

examples of saints long dead. Here the readers are urged to be among the faithful.

Some will be rejected, cursed and burned (6:8), but "we are persuaded better things of you" (6:9)! Let each believer be fully informed regarding the destiny of deserters and apostates. Let him tremble before the wrath of a righteous God. But let him then be encouraged and consoled and strengthened, lest he become discouraged and fall to another of Satan's devices. This is the true style of exhortation, and Hebrews is above all a "word of exhortation" (13:22).

CHAPTER ELEVEN

11:1. In this chapter our author will illustrate that faith which saves the soul by pointing to men and women from Jewish history who possessed it. He begins, however, with a statement concerning this saving faith, which some have called its definition.

Faith is, on the one hand, **the substance** or confidence or courageous assurance (see the same word at 3:14) **of things hoped for.** This term expresses the sense well of the Hebrew word for faith used throughout the Old Testament. It is that confident and assured trust in God which enables one to endure with patience while moving toward the object of his hope.

Faith is, on the other hand, the **evidence** or proof, the absolute conviction, **of things not seen** with the physical eyes. This terminology expresses the sense of the Greek word for faith used in the New Testament. Saving faith, however, in every age and among all men, involves both these elements. It

> is its own proof of the existence and active energy of unseen facts and realities, and able by its own immediate intuitions to dispense with the evidence of the senses and laborious proofs of reason. It carries the imperious conviction of the truth it holds within itself (Delitzsch).

2 For by it the elders obtained a good report.

Putting it more simply, such faith "is convinced of future good because it knows that the good for which it hopes already exists invisibly in God" (Barrett). In that conviction, faith rises to meet great occasions, accomplishes mighty works through God's power, and endures every kind of suffering for the sake of Him whose voice it has heard and whose reward it has seen.

11:2. By it the elders or honorable men of the past **obtained a good report** or were well-attested by God. This general term will include heroes of faith from Abel the son of Adam through the Maccabean martyrs of the second century before Christ.

It was common practice among Greek orators, as among speakers now, to illustrate particular traits by calling attention to individuals in whom they have been particularly apparent. When Mattathias, the priestly father of the Maccabean brothers, encouraged his sons on his deathbed he said,

> Now my children, be zealous for the Law, and give your lives for the covenant of your fathers. And call to mind the deeds of the fathers which they did in their generations; that ye may receive great glory and an everlasting name (I Maccabees 2:50-51).

He then reminded them of the faith and deeds of Abraham, Joseph, Phinehas, Joshua, Caleb, David, Elijah, Daniel and his three friends.

Another Jewish writing began with the following words a seven-chapter description of the merits of good men from Enoch to a Maccabean priest named Simeon:

> Let me now hymn the praises of men of piety, of our fathers in their generations. No little glory did the Most High allot them, and they were great from the days of old (Sirach 44:1-2).

Our author is not unique in naming famous men. He is alone in calling attention to the clear quality of saving faith which has exemplified all who truly pleased God. This verse may give a capsule illustration of the first part of faith's description in verse one. These **elders** were men who maintained a confidence and courage and assurance toward God in the face of whatever circumstance they encountered.

3 Through faith we understand that the worlds were framed by the word of God, so that things which are seen were not made of things which do appear.

4 By faith Abel offered unto God a more excellent sacrifice than Cain, by which he obtained witness that he

---

11:3. Through this same kind of faith we understand the origin of the universe although we have no physical evidence to support our understanding. Paul uses **understand** in a similar statement in Romans 1:20. Here is just one example of the second part of the definition found in verse one.

The worlds (see 1:2) here refer to the space-time universe which is known by sensory perception, although the particular word literally means "ages." All that is now seen was **framed** or came into being by the spoken **word of God**. Nothing came originally from what philosophers would call the phenomenal, but from God's own invisible word and will.

The **word** of God here is not the same as in John 1:1ff. John uses a word which includes both rationality or thought and the speech by which that is expressed. Our author uses a term which emphasizes the act of speaking. The former may be included in his remark that what we see did not come from what is apparent, and in the implication that it came from the mind and thoughts of God — which are invisible — by means of the spoken word of God.

If Moses saw a pattern of the true tabernacle in heaven before he built the one on earth (8:5; 9:1), it is not surprising that the visible creation should have come from the thoughts of God and in the absence of any visible "stuff."

On creation through God's spoken word, see also Genesis 1, 2; Psalm 33:6, 9. The important point is that **through faith** we **understand** this, and that we may have the same **proof** or **evidence** through faith that one might seek through physical senses.

11:4. The first example of faith is **Abel**, who **by it offered a sacrifice** which **God** regarded as **more excellent than** that offered by his brother **Cain**. The story is told in

was righteous, God testifying of his gifts: and by it he being

---

Genesis 4:3-7. A number of suggestions have been made as to why Abel's offering pleased God when Cain's did not.

Cain brought his fruit but Abel brought his firstfruits. Abel's blood-offering may have signified a realization of his need for forgiveness, while Cain's offering of produce showed no such insight or humility. Others have concluded that God prescribed the specific offering desired and that we have a simple contrast between obedience and disobedience. Our author says only that Abel's acceptance was due to his faith. There seems to be a simpler explanation of these words than any yet mentioned.

Faith which successfully approaches God by nature involves the heart. Our writer urges that the heart not be hardened (3:8), or evil and unbelieving (3:12) when judged by God's word (4:12). It is rather to be inscribed with God's laws (8:10; 10:16), sincere, with full assurance of faith (10:22) and strengthened by grace (13:9). The text here says that Abel's offering was accepted because he presented it out of faith, and the Old Testament indicates a distinction between the hearts of Abel and his brother Cain (Genesis 4:7).

Calvin pointed to this factor in his comment that Abel's sacrifice was accepted "because he himself was graciously accepted," and Proverbs 15:8 affirms the same principle. As all righteous men of all time, Abel pleased God through faith. This faith which guided all his life caused him to be accepted, and the occasion of his offering gave God opportunity to acknowledge the acceptance of his faith. This was in contrast to Cain's rejection, because of disbelief.

It is even here the case that faith comes by hearing the word of God, but Abel's faith responded to God's word in general and regularly, not simply on this occasion. The key to his accepted offering is not the offering itself but his heart. God was pleased to accept the offering because of the faith which prompted the man who brought it.

By the same faith Abel obtained witness from God that he was righteous. If one construes the which here as referring to the sacrifice instead of the faith, the point remains

dead yet speaketh.

5 By faith Enoch was translated that he should not see death; and was not found, because God had translated him: for before his translation he had this testimony, that he pleased God.

---

unchanged. For, if by the sacrifice Abel obtained witness from God, it was only in God's testimony that he was known to be righteous — but he was righteous because of his faith.

That Abel was **righteous** is stated by our Lord Himself (Matthew 23:35) as well as by the apostle John (I John 3:12). Josephus also states that Cain and Abel

> were pleased with different courses of life; for Abel, the younger, was a lover of righteousness, and, believing that God was present at all his actions, he excelled in virtue. . . . But Cain was not only very wicked in other respects, but was wholly intent upon getting.

God testified that Abel was **righteous** by receiving **his gifts.** Whether He indicated this reception by a divine word or by sending fire upon the altar (see Leviticus 9:23-24; Judges 6:21ff; 13:19-23; I Kings 18:30-39; II Chronicles 7:1) we are not told.

Though Abel had been long **dead** even when Hebrews was written, **by** his **faith** he **yet speaketh.** His message is not only a cry to God for vengeance (Genesis 4:10; Hebrews 12:24), but is particularly a word to all God's people that they may find divine favor through faith.

11:5. If Abel died as a result of his faith, the next witness found life through his. **By faith Enoch** was **translated** when God took him (Genesis 5:24; see II Kings 2:3, 5, 10), which our author interprets as meaning that **he** did not **see death.** When Enoch's associates searched for him **he was not found** (see II Kings 2:15-17). But **before his translation** Enoch **had** received **this testimony** or witness **that he pleased God.**

The Greek Old Testament says that Enoch "was well-pleasing to God," where the Hebrew text says he "walked with God." These terms are applied by the Old Testament to Noah as well as to Enoch, but to no other man (Genesis

6 But without faith it is impossible to please him: for he that cometh to God must believe that he is, and that he is a rewarder of them that diligently seek him.

7 By faith Noah, being warned of God of things not seen as yet, moved with fear, prepared an ark to the saving of his house; by the which he condemned the world, and became heir of the righteousness which is by faith.

6:9). Jude indicates that Enoch's contemporaries were anything but pleasing to God (verses 14-15), and one piece of uninspired Jewish literature had him "caught away lest wickedness should change his understanding or guile deceive his soul" (Wisdom 4:11). Again, what is important is that Enoch pleased God through his faith.

11:6. Although the Old Testament does not state that Enoch was a man of faith, our writer argues that he must have been. For without faith it is impossible to please God, yet Scripture says that Enoch did. What is true of Enoch is true in general. Any person who comes to God (the same Greek word used in Hebrews 4:16; 7:25 and 10:1, 22 of approaching God) must believe or have a two-fold faith. First, that God is or exists; second, that he becomes a rewarder to those who diligently seek him by faith.

Both these are in keeping with the nature of faith as described in verse one. Faith believes that God is, although He is not seen, and that He will give those seeking Him the reward for which they hope. Only with such faith is God pleased; He has no pleasure in those who draw back in disbelief (10:38). Those who received this epistle needed just such a faith if they were to receive their reward (10:35). Those who read it today need the same.

11:7. Noah was also a man of faith. Like Abel, he was righteous; like Enoch, he walked with God or pleased Him (Genesis 6:9). When warned of God Noah prepared an ark, for his faith provided evidence of things not seen as yet. He moved with godly fear or piety (see the same word at 5:7; 12:28), itself a companion of faith, which resulted in the saving of his house.

By faith, Noah condemned the world which did not have faith. He became an heir of the only righteousness God

8 By faith Abraham, when he was called to go out into
a place which he should after receive for an inheritance,
obeyed; and he went out, not knowing whither he went.

9 By faith he sojourned in the land of promise, as
in a strange country, dwelling in tabernacles with Isaac and
Jacob, the heirs with him of the same promise:

---

recognizes, that which is according to faith. Noah was saved
by faith. His faith showed itself by acting in assurance of the
unseen, through confidence in the God who had promised.

11:8. The next five verses speak of Abraham's faith,
noted by Old Testament writers (Genesis 15:6; Nehemiah
9:8) as well as New (Romans 4; Galatians 3:6-9). Our writer
has already discussed Abraham twice (he is mentioned in
2:16); once in connection with God's faithfulness (6:13-15)
and once in giving historical background to Melchizedek
(7:1-10). Here Abraham's faith is in the spotlight.

By faith Abraham obeyed the call of God to go out, not
knowing where he would go. He knew only that God had
commanded. "Faith and obedience are inseparable in man's
relation to God." Abraham "would not have obeyed the divine call had he not taken God at his word; his obedience
was the outward evidence of his inward faith" (Bruce).

Abraham was to receive a promise of the land as an inheritance, but that promise was not given until after he had
initially obeyed (Genesis 12:1-7). The promise concerning
an inheritance was itself a reward for his initial faith, not
the original motive for his obedience. That rested on his
faith alone.

11:9. By faith Abraham sojourned or lived as a stranger
who was passing through a strange country, although in
fact he was in the land which according to God's promise
would some day belong to his descendants. He lived with
Isaac, who was born when Abraham was 100 years old
(Genesis 21:5), and Jacob, born when he was 160 (Genesis
25:26), for fifteen years (Genesis 25:7) in tabernacles or
tents.

As semi-nomads (Genesis 26:12; 33:17) the patriarchs
did not settle for the luxuries of any city around them. The

10 For he looked for a city which hath foundations, whose builder and maker is God.

11 Through faith also Sarah herself received strength to conceive seed, and was delivered of a child when she was past age, because she judged him faithful who had promised.

---

metropolitan areas of Sodom and Gomorrah were by no means alone in Palestine and Syria of Abraham's day. Jericho had been a fortified city already for more than 5,000 years. Yet the patriarchs remained intentional strangers, looking for a special kind of city which only God could prepare.

11:10. Abraham, and apparently Isaac and Jacob as well (see verses 13-16), **looked for** the **city which hath** the **foundations**. Both definite articles are present in the original, adding emphasis to the uniqueness of the city for which they searched. The following verses tell us that they were trusting God for a home in the heavenly city. This verse calls it the city with the foundations, **whose builder** or craftsman or architect **and maker** or constructor **is God.**

In addition to other references in Hebrews (12:22; 13:14), the new or heavenly Jerusalem is mentioned in Galatians (4:25-26) and Revelation (3:12; chapters 21, 22). At times it is a present reality, distinguished from earthly Jerusalem as the spiritual is distinguished from the physical, and is discernable by faith. At the same time, it is to be distinguished in a temporal sense as the inheritance not-yet-given which awaits the people of God. In Hebrews, notes Bruce, "it is the heavenly Jerusalem, the commonwealth of God in the spiritual and eternal order, now effectively made accessible by the completion of Christ's high-priestly work, to which all the men and women of faith come to be enrolled as free citizens" (see also Philippians 3:20).

11:11. The text used by the King James translators notes that **by faith Abraham's** wife **Sarah** was enabled to bear a son although **past** the normal **age.** A problem arises here, however, because the Greek word translated **conceive seed** is not the word for the mother's part in conception at all, but the father's. In addition, Sarah is pictured in the Old Testament, not as believing God's promise, but laughing

12 Therefore sprang there even of one, and him as good as dead, so many as the stars of the sky in multitude, and as the sand which is by the sea shore innumerable.

13 These all died in faith, not having received the

---

at it in scorn and disbelief (Genesis 18:12-15). Finally, the statement that Sarah **was delivered of a child** is not in the better Greek manuscripts or the later English versions.

A solution may not be far away. The original words here represented as **Sarah herself received strength to conceive seed,** may, by remarking the vowels, be translated: "He also, with Sarah, received strength to begat a child, when he was past age." This reading is suggested in the margin of the Westcott and Hort Greek text and is noted with approval in the lexicons translated by Thayer and by Arndt and Gingrich. It does not do violence to the original text, either, for vowels in it were not marked. This reading not only accounts for the particular Greek word used, it fits the facts of the Old Testament and makes the present passage far more readable. **By faith** Abraham went out (verse eight), sojourned (verse nine), with Sarah had a son (verse 11), and offered Isaac (verse 17).

The fulfillment of this promise, impossible by human calculations, became possible **by** the **faith** of Abraham. He exemplified that highest quality of faith which judges God to be **faithful** in all that He has **promised,** and acts accordingly.

11:12. Not only Isaac, but eventually a **multitude** as numerous as the **stars** in the sky (Genesis 15:5; 22:17) or the grains of **sand** by the shore (Genesis 22:17) came from the **one** man Abraham (Isaiah 51:1-2; Ezekiel 33:24). To this add that he was **as good as dead** so far as producing offspring when Isaac was promised. The text literally says that he had long been dead in this sense. Paul uses the same form of this word in Romans 4:19. There he insists that saving faith is faith in a God who is able to raise the dead, and he develops that point with reference to Christian faith in the gospel concerning Christ (see also verse 19 in this chapter).

11:13. **These** sojourning worthies — Abraham (and Sarah), Isaac and Jacob — **all died** just as they had lived, in

promises, but having seen them afar off, and were persuaded of them, and embraced them, and confessed that they were strangers and pilgrims on the earth.

14 For they that say such things declare plainly that they seek a country.

15 And truly, if they had been mindful of that country from whence they came out, they might have had opportunity to have returned.

---

the sphere where faith is the motivating principle. Although they did not during their lifetime receive the object of the **promises** given them, by faith they had **seen them** as if from a distance. Their faith saw what was invisible and the conviction it produced caused them to react with certain assurance. They **embraced** what they saw (literally "greeted" or "saluted"), and happily **confessed that they were strangers and pilgrims** — not only in that land but **on the earth** itself (see verse ten).

Abraham confessed that he was a stranger and pilgrim (Genesis 23:4), as did Jacob (Genesis 47:9). David, a later man of faith, made the same confession in his day (Psalm 39:12; 119:19; I Chronicles 29:15). Peter urges Christians to have the same attitude (I Peter 1:17; 2:11), as does our writer in making the present point.

11:14. **They that say** that they are strangers and pilgrims on this earth **declare plainly** that they are looking for a **country** or fatherland of their own. The patriarchs did say **such things** and we may know that was their quest.

11:15. The country they sought was not one from which **they came out,** whether Haran or Chaldea. When on one occasion a servant suggested that Isaac return to Haran to acquire a wife, Abraham was urgent in insisting against it (Genesis 24:5-8). God had called him away from that country; his mind was not set on it and he did not **return** even when he **had opportunity.** These men were pilgrims, not leaving a former home only, but travelling toward a future one. They were immigrants to the heavenly city, as well as emigrants from one on earth.

**16 But now they desire a better country, that is, an
heavenly: wherefore God is not ashamed to be called their
God: for he hath prepared for them a city.**

17 By faith Abraham, when he was tried, offered up

11:16. They wanted a **heavenly** country **better** than any
earth could provide. They were not perfect mortals by any
standard, but they were men who trusted God and took Him
at His word. For this reason **he is not ashamed to be called
their God** (Genesis 28:13; Exodus 3:6; see Mark 12:26-27).
For the same reason He **has prepared** that heavenly **city**
for which they looked during their lives.

Just as the true sabbath rest is fulfilled only in the
eternal realm of realities entered after death by the faithful
(4:1-11; Revelation 14:13), so the faith-pilgrim finds his city
only in the dimension of perfected existence.

An unknown writer from perhaps the third century after
Christ had the same thought in mind when he described
Christians in these words.

> They live in their own homelands, but as foreigners.
> They share in everything as citizens, but endure every-
> thing as aliens. Every foreign country is their home-
> land, but every homeland is a strange country to
> them. They spend their time on the earth, but their
> citizenship is really in heaven (Epistle to Diognetus,
> my translation).

11:17. It was also **by faith** that **Abraham** was offering
Isaac, having already **offered** him in his own heart and
mind, when an angel of God stopped him short of the actual
deed. The story is given in Genesis 22:1-14. Jewish traditions had Isaac 23, 25 or even 37 years old at the time, and
credited him with the same faith as his father, but the Genesis account leaves the impression that Isaac was much
younger.

The tense of the first verb **offered up** indicates an action completed in the past with results carrying into the
present. Abraham's faith was so real that he regarded Isaac
as already having been offered. Apparently, God did as well.
But Abraham's faith was not limited to his mind, for he was
in the process of carrying out this act (as the tense of the
second **offered up** suggests) when stopped by God. Faith

Isaac: and he that had received the promises offered up his only begotten son,

18 Of whom it was said, That in Isaac shall thy seed be called:

19 Accounting that God was able to raise him up, even from the dead; from whence also he received him in a figure.

---

is what justifies, not the act it prompts; yet justifying faith will always be acting in obedience to God.

Scripture refers to this incident as a test by which Abraham's faith was **tried** (Genesis 22:1, 12). An ancient Jewish work called The Book of Jubilees told of a confrontation behind the scenes between God and a demon, details borrowed, no doubt, from the Biblical story of Job.

11:18. There could be no doubt as to the crisis: it was to be in or through **Isaac** that the race which would **be called** the **seed** of Abraham would have its origin (Genesis 21:12). The test of Abraham's faith lay in the realization that God's **promises** to him depended on this very **only begotten** son whom God now commanded to be offered as a sacrifice. What does one do when God's promises seem to contradict His clear commands? Abraham's example would say that faith suspends human reasoning and obeys, trusting that God is both able and faithful to carry out His promises.

11:19. If God could **raise** one up **from the dead** by a miraculous birth to aged parents (verse 12; Romans 4:17-22), He **was** certainly **able** to raise Isaac from the death Abraham was now commanded to inflict. This much Abraham knew, and he seems to have believed that God would do this very thing (Genesis 22:5).

Because Isaac was already dead in Abraham's faithful mind (see verse 17), our author says that is what did happen; not literally, but **in a figure.** Abraham's faith was approved. He **received** his son alive as a reward.

Because **figure** here is literally "parable," some have taken the phrase to mean that what happened to Isaac was a figure or parable of Jesus who was to come. Whether or not that was in our author's mind, a number of parallels are apparent. Isaac was Abraham's only begotten son (verse 17;

20 By faith Isaac blessed Jacob and Esau concerning
things to come.

21 By faith Jacob, when he was a dying, blessed both
the sons of Joseph; and worshipped, leaning upon the top

---

see John 3:16). He was a child of promise through whom
God would bless the world. He was born of a miraculous conception.

Isaac carried the wood for his own death, as Jesus carried His own cross. Isaac was received back as from the
dead, as our Lord was in fact. In Isaac's place, God provided
a ram for the sacrifice, caught in a thicket by his horns.
Jesus Himself was the Lamb of God, but died with a crown
of thorns on His head. Both events involve a test of faith.
Man is now asked to place all hope of salvation in the
crucified and risen Jesus, a proposition as troubling to human
reason as the dilemma faced by Abraham.

11:20. **By faith** this same **Isaac,** when he was old and
blind, **blessed** his sons **Jacob** (Genesis 27:26-29; 28:1-4) **and
Esau** (Genesis 27:39-40) **concerning things** which were
to come in the distant future. These blessings involved the
fortunes of two nations, Israel and Edom, and they came to
pass as foretold. That Isaac spoke by faith implies more
in the blessings than a fatherly prediction. What he said must
have been based on a word from God.

The measure of faith required from Isaac is seen in the
very circumstance of the blessing. Jacob had reversed the
ordinary prophecy through common deceit, and the blessings
were given unwillfully by Isaac. Yet Isaac was confident
that God would carry out His purposes.

God is all-knowing and all-powerful, and faith trusts Him
to accomplish His will in spite of all human obstacles. No
circumstance may arise through human sin which God can
not use for His own glory. This is the confident conviction
of every one who believes that God is and that He becomes
a rewarder to those who seek Him.

11:21. Many years later, **Jacob** acted **by faith** when he
blessed Ephraim and Manasseh, the two **sons of Joseph**

of his staff.

22 By faith Joseph, when he died, made mention of the departing of the children of Israel; and gave commandment concerning his bones.

23 By faith Moses, when he was born, was hid three

(Genesis 48:1-22). See the comments regarding the patriarchal blessing above.

The same faith was evident in Jacob when he made Joseph swear to have him buried some day in the land of promise, then leaned in reverence **upon the top of his** pilgrim's **staff** and **worshipped** the God of his fathers (Genesis 47:29-31).

God's promise to Abraham had included affliction in a strange country, but also a great deliverance after four generations (Genesis 15:13-16). In that promise alone Jacob placed all his confidence now. In spite of "the exhaustion of approaching death, he summoned all his bodily powers, and placed his aged limbs as well as he could in the position of profoundest adoration" (Delitzsch).

It may be noticed that Genesis has "bed" where our author has "staff." The same consonants in Hebrew may be either; our author is using a Greek translation which had "staff." The faith of Jacob remains the same in either case, and that is the point.

The writer of Hebrews may reverse the chronological order of the two events in this verse for smoother transition from Isaac's blessing (verse 20) to Jacob's blessing (verse 21), and from Jacob's death-bed (verse 21) to Joseph's (verse 22).

11:22. Dying Joseph acted **by faith** when he spoke of **the** divinely promised **departing of the children of Israel** (see notes on verse 21), **and gave** a **commandment concerning** the future burial of **his bones** (Genesis 50:24-25). His faith in God's promise was vindicated many years later when his bones were carried up out of Egypt (Exodus 13:19) and laid to rest at Shechem (Joshua 24:32).

11:23. **By faith, Moses,** who has been commended already

months of his parents, because they saw he was a proper
child; and they were not afraid of the king's commandment.

**24 By faith Moses, when he was come to years, re-
fused to be called the son of Pharaoh's daughter;**

---

for faithfulness in God's house (3:2, 5), **was hid three
months** (Exodus 2:2) **by his parents** Amram and Jochebed
(Exodus 6:20). Their act was in violation of **the king's commandment** that Hebrew male infants should be destroyed
(Exodus 1:22). To say that Moses was **a proper child** is to
say he was urbane, stately or well-favored (see Acts 7:20).
Jewish tradition said that Moses' parents were informed of
God's plans for Moses, through either a dream of Amram or
a prophetic utterance by Moses' sister Miriam. Scripture
states simply that they acted from faith.

11:24. **When** Moses **was** mature or **come to years,** he
acted **by faith** and **refused to be called the son of Pharoah's
daughter,** by whom he had been adopted as an infant (Exodus 2:9-10). The refusal may have taken the form of a
dramatic confrontation or it may have been by identification
with the enslaved Hebrews through incidents such as that recorded in Exodus 2:11-12 (see also Acts 7:23-25).

The identity of **Pharoah's daughter** must remain a present mystery. The designation "Pharoah" is of no help, since
it was not a personal name but the ancient royal title
meaning "The one who lives in the great house." Josephus
says the Pharoah's daughter was named Thermuthis, and
the Jewish Book of Jubilees called her Tharmuth. Both are
names of a daughter of Rameses II, who lived during the
thirteenth century before Christ. Another daughter of Rameses II, Meri, has also been suggested as the princess of
Exodus.

Conservative scholarship has generally preferred an
earlier date for Moses, and some writers have suggested that
this princess was Hatshepsut, a powerful daughter of Thut-
mose I. Hatshepsut later became "king" herself, and even
wore the ceremonial beard of the pharoah. She ruled during
the fifteenth century before Christ.

Our historical curiosity must wait for further evidence
from archaeology, but our appreciation of the faith of Moses

25 Choosing rather to suffer affliction with the people of God, than to enjoy the pleasures of sin for a season;

26 Esteeming the reproach of Christ greater riches than the treasures in Egypt: for he had respect unto the recompense of the reward.

---

remains unaffected. Whenever he lived, his worldly position warred against his faith. To his eternal credit Moses trusted God instead of appearances, and of his alternatives our author now speaks.

11:25. Moses could have known a powerful position in Egypt, perhaps even becoming Pharoah. Instead he cast his lot with a race of slaves. His faith looked behind the scenes and calculated it better to suffer affliction with the people of the eternally-existent and rewarding God than to enjoy all the conceivable pleasures of sin which were temporary (see this same word at II Corinthians 4:18). By faith, Moses "looked through the deceptive appearances of worldly good things, to their inward and essential nothingness, and to their fearful end" (Delitzsch).

11:26. The treasures of Egypt were fantastic, as demonstrated by a few small caches uncovered in certain royal tombs. The treasures of King "Tut" (Tutankhaton, fourteenth century before Christ) are well known; that much or more might have belonged to Moses. But faith appraised the alternatives and pronounced reproaches with God's people to be the greater riches!

Moses chose the reproaches (see 10:33) of Christ. Suffering accepted for God's sake binds together saints of both testaments and identifies them all with Christ (Philippians 1:29; Colossians 1:24; II Timothy 2:10). David so spoke in Psalm 69:7-9, in words later seen to refer also to Christ (John 2:17; Romans 15:3). In another psalm, Ethan spoke of his sufferings as for the sake of God's anointed one (the literal meaning of "Christ," 89:50-51). Moses endured reproaches, as Christ was to do; he was a type of Christ (Deuteronomy 18:18; Acts 3:20-23). His suffering was one link in the great chain of events by which God directed history to its focal point in Christ.

27 By faith he forsook Egypt, not fearing the wrath
of the king: for he endured, as seeing him who is invisible.

28 Through faith he kept the passover, and the
sprinkling of blood, lest he that destroyed the firstborn

11:27. **By faith** Moses **forsook Egypt** for Midian (Exodus 2:15). Lest the Exodus account be misunderstood, our
author adds that this flight was not prompted by **the wrath of
the king.** Like his parents before him (verse 23), Moses was
well aware of Pharoah's wrath, but also like them he acted
through positive faith in God and not through fear. Fear
might have led a slave rebellion — which would have been
crushed at once. Faith quietly retreated to the desert to be
molded forty years for God's great deliverance.

In this particular crisis and thereafter, Moses **endured**
the **consequences** of his faith by looking toward God **who is
invisible.** Again we are reminded that faith believes that
God is and that He is a rewarder of those who seek Him.
The faith of Moses stood against the unbelief of Pharoah,
who Philo says "did not acknowledge any deity apart from
those that could be seen." The plagues on Egypt were
judgments against its many visible gods (Exodus 12:12).

Some relate this verse to the Exodus rather than to
Moses' earlier flight to Midian, but at least four objections
may be raised to that view. First, the order here is reversed.
The Passover preceded the Exodus but is mentiond in the
verse following this one. Second, our writer does not mention
the faith of Israel here, as he does regarding the Red Sea
(verse 29) and as one might expect if this refers to the
Exodus. Third, Pharoah of the Exodus was not the king from
whom Moses fled, yet our author has to deny that fear
prompted the flight under consideration (Exodus 2:23).
Fourth, Israel did not leave Egypt under fear, but at the urging of Pharoah and the Egyptians (Exodus 12:31-33).

11:28. **By faith** (the word here is exactly that translated
"by faith" elsewhere in the chapter), **Moses kept the passover** for the first time and left it as a perpetual celebration
(Exodus 12:1-20). Faith prompted the **sprinkling of** the lamb's

should touch them.

29 By faith they passed through the Red Sea as by dry land: which the Egyptians assaying to do were drowned.

---

blood; it was rewarded in Israel's deliverance when **the firstborn** of Egypt's men and animals were **destroyed** by God (Exodus 12:21-30).

Jesus instituted the Lord's Supper at a passover meal. His selection of bread and fruit of the vine as the elements of His covenant meal also demonstrates the continuity between old and new testaments.

John's Gospel presents Jesus' death against a background of the slaying of passover lambs in the temple (John 19:31, 36). Paul makes the unleavened bread of passover week a type representing moral purity among Christians, whose Lamb is Christ (I Corinthians 5:6-8). Our author does not use passover typology. He stresses the Day of Atonement and its perfect fulfillment in the self-offering of Christ. For additional references on Christ as God's Lamb, see notes on 9:24.

11:29. The Israelites were represented by Moses in the previous verse. Here **they** are mentioned as a company. It is striking that examples of faith are drawn from individuals, usually persons who were faithful when all around them were not. The nation is used to illustrate disbelief (3:9-11; 3:16-4:11; I Corinthians 10:1-12). This great moment of Israel's faith immediately precedes forty years of unbelief in the wilderness.

By faith Israel **passed through the** midst of the divided **Red Sea** (Exodus 14:21-22), though God divided the sea with a strong east wind which came at a signal from Moses (Exodus 14:21). The Egyptians lacked faith, (literally) "made a trial of" the sea, and **were drowned.**

The Hebrew Old Testament calls this the Sea of Reeds. English versions generally agree with the Greek Old Testament in calling it the Red Sea. Exodus 14:2 indicates that the crossing took place at a northern extension of what is now the Gulf of Suez. This mighty act of divine deliverance was immediately celebrated in a song of praise (Exodus 15:

30 By faith the walls of Jericho fell down, after they were compassed about seven days.

31 By faith the harlot Rahab perished not with them that believed not, when she had received the spies with peace.

1-21); still later it was used to represent God's great power to accomplish His covenant purposes (Isaiah 11:15-16; 51: 10-11). Paul used this crossing as a type of Christian baptism, and argued from it that those once in fellowship with God may forfeit their blessing through loss of faith (I Corinthians 10:1ff).

11:30. The capture of Jericho (Joshua six) involved what we call psychological warfare; the inhabitants must have been terrified after six days of encirclement by a silent army who marched behind blowing trumpets. But the walls fell down on the seventh day — and that by the faith which prompted the past week's strange behavior. On Israel's part the six days of marching demonstrated the perseverance of true faith — an element close to our writer's mind as he pens this chapter (10:35-39; 12:1, 3).

An archaeologist named Garstang thought he had uncovered the very walls which fell before Joshua, but dating based on later work of Kathleen Kenyon made that identification very unlikely. Such matters are of interest, but the truthfulness of the biblical story does not depend on the excavator's spade. The same God whom Israel's faith touched that day thousands of years ago stands now behind our written account of that event, and the same kind of faith which trusted His direct word then places confidence now in His word that is written.

11:31. When the walls of Jericho fell and Israel stormed the city, Rahab and her family were the only survivors (Joshua 6:22-25). Her salvation was the result of her faith, which had been demonstrated earlier in hiding the two Israelite spies (Joshua 2). Her act was of faith because she had heard of God's past deeds for Israel and she behaved from a reverent recognition of His power and purposes (Joshua 2:10-11).

Rahab is contrasted here with them that believed not. The word translated "believe" here implies obedience that

32   And what shall I more say? for the time would fail me to tell of Gideon, and of Barak, and of Samson, and of

---

comes from a persuasion of faith (the same word is used at 3:18). James uses Rahab as an illustration of that saving faith which does not merely profess but obeys (2:25). Clement of Rome, an early Christian author whose work was not inspired, used Rahab as an example of hospitality and faith (I Clement 12:1).

Some pious Jews of antiquity tried to make Rahab an innkeeper or a seller of food, instead of a **harlot,** but the word used in both Old and New Testaments demands that she be just that. Nor is this the word for a cultic or pagan temple prostitute, but an ordinary harlot. In spite of her former way of life, Rahab was transformed through the power of faith. She later was to marry a Hebrew named Salmon to become a chosen vessel in the ancestry of our Lord (Matthew 1:5).

11:32. Using a Greek phrase common to orators, our author notes that his **time would fail** if he detailed every example of faith, and draws his list to a close.

The first four names are selected from the period of the Judges, and carry the Old Testament story from the time of Joshua to the time of the kings. **Gideon** delivered Israel from marauding Midianities who used the speed of camels to make their plundering attacks (Judges 6-8). Gideon is also called Jerubbaal (Judges 6:32).

As Deborah's war-captain, **Barak** shared in the deliverance of the northwestern tribes from a confederacy of Canaanite kings who used chariots long before they were a common vehicle of war. The story in Judges 4-5 does not indicate Barak's faith, unless it is to be seen in his agreement to assist Deborah with prospects of no personal glory (4: 8-9). Chronologically Barak comes before Gideon, but in importance the order is here reversed.

The exploits of **Samson** against Philistine occupation-troops are familiar to the Bible student (Judges 13-16).

Jephthah; of David also, and Samuel, and of the prophets:

Samson's faith was not always strong or active, but it came to the fore on the occasion of his death.

Jephthah was instrumental in delivering the eastern tribes from Ammon (Judges 11-12). Though he is now remembered chiefly for a rash vow, his general behavior was grounded in a knowledge of God's past acts on behalf of Israel and a confidence that He would act once more for His own people (11:14-27). Jephthah also illustrates the fact that God may use ignoble individuals to accomplish great things (Judges 11:1-3).

It is possible that these four individuals were grouped together soon after their own times. First Samuel 12:11 speaks of Jerubbaal (Gideon) and Bedan (the Greek and Syriac versions have Barak) and Jephthah and Samuel (the Syriac version has Samson, but that seems to be a change that is unwarranted).

Time would fail, indeed, to give details of the faith of **David** (I Samuel 16-31; II Samuel; I Chronicles 11-29). The man after God's own heart (Acts 13:22) who served God's purpose in his own generation (Acts 13:36) must have been characterized by exceptional faith, for without faith it is impossible to please God at all.

Samuel was the last of the judges and the first of a chain of **prophets** who would instruct Israel through the rest of the Old Testament period (I Samuel 19:20). Although he preceded David, he is here placed more naturally with **the prophets** who followed him. Samuel's own birth was in answer to a prayer of faith (I Samuel 1:10-20), and his personal ministry early included a total trust in the word God revealed to him (I Samuel 3).

The prophets include Elijah, Elisha, Micaiah and other non-writing prophets, as well as the sixteen whose books bear their names. One does not have to look far to be impressed by their faith. He needs only to consider the mighty works of Elijah and Elisha, the patient and trying service of Hosea or Jeremiah, the holy boldness of Micaiah or Amos or Daniel, the unquestioning obedience of Ezekiel,

33 Who through faith subdued kingdoms, wrought
righteousness, obtained promises, stopped the mouths of
lions,

34 Quenched the violence of fire, escaped the edge of
the sword, out of weakness were made strong, waxed valiant

---

or the confident reliance which Habakkuk expresses so
beautifully in his poetic third chapter. These men all, along
with a host of God's holy ones whose faith will be celebrated
only in the resurrection, eloquently illustrate the many-
faceted qualities of that faith which is unto the saving of
the soul.

11:33. **Through faith** men have **subdued kingdoms.**
Joshua, the judges and David come to mind at once. Others
have **wrought righteousness** by the public administration
of divine justice. This is noted of Samuel (I Samuel 12:4)
and David (II Samuel 8:15; Psalm 101). **Faith** has **obtained**
the fulfillment as well as the word of **promises:** of the Exodus, of Canaan's possession, of great territories, of God's
care and protection of Jerusalem, of a captivity that ended
as predicted and a return home.

Faith has **stopped the mouths of lions,** by death (Judges
14:5-6; I Samuel 17:34-36), but especially when Daniel had
been delivered to hungry lions by his enemies and God delivered him from their jaws (Daniel 6).

11:34. Faith has sometimes **quenched the violence of
fire,** most notably in the case of Shadrach, Meshach and
Abednego (Daniel 3). Peter's mention of "fiery trials" may
suggest that such persecution was a possibility in the case of
those who first read this epistle (I Peter 4:12).

Elijah (I Kings 19), Elisha (II Kings 6) and Jeremiah
(Jeremiah 36) all **escaped the edge of the sword** by faith,
but others by faith met the steel (Hebrews 11:37).

Out of weakness men and women of faith **were made
strong.** Gideon was the most insignificant member of his
family, but God used him mightily. Neither Saul nor David
claimed personal merit when God called for service. Both
responded to that call in faith, and in personal weakness
found God's strength. Others already discussed in this

in fight, turned to flight the armies of the aliens.

35 Women received their dead raised to life again: and others were tortured, not accepting deliverance; that they might obtain a better resurrection:

---

chapter were enabled by faith to accomplish what would otherwise have been impossible.

God has never depended on numbers, nor has He valued man's appraisals of strength and weakness (see Deuteronomy 32:30; Leviticus 26:8; Joshua 23:10; II Corinthians 1:9-10; 12:9-10). To consider the examples in this chapter is more frequently than not to see God working in spite of the very instruments He chooses to use, overcoming men's own weaknesses and mistakes to bring about His eventual glory. This lesson is always needed in the church, for men constantly face the temptation to view life through human values rather than with the clear and certain lens of faith.

By faith other **waxed valiant in fight** and **turned the armies of the aliens to flight.** Old Testament characters could be adduced here, but these terms also fit the heroic men of faith who lived between the testaments. The book of I Maccabees is not inspired, but it tells of numerous victories which faith brought the sons of Mattathias in their godly struggle against the pagan Syrian ruler Antiochus Epiphanes.

11:35. **Women** who had lost loved ones **received** them **to life again** through the power of faith. We think of the widow of Zarephath (I Kings 17:17ff) and the Shunemite woman (II Kings 4:17ff); perhaps there were others.

Tortured here translates a word which describes quite literally an extremely cruel persecution in which an individual was stretched on a rack then beaten to death. Second Maccabees is not quite so reliable as the first book, but it tells of a godly scribe named Eleazar who died in this very manner for his faith in Jehovah (6:18-31).

When Eleazar was captured, he was offered **deliverance** if he would eat swine's flesh. This he refused, in hope of **a better resurrection.** Whether our author has him in mind

36   And others had trial of cruel mockings and scourg-

---

or not, Eleazar's dying words are characteristic of those who
are intended here. "The Lord, who hath holy knowledge,
understandeth that although I might have been freed from
death, I endure cruel pains in my body from scourging and
suffer this gladly in my soul, because I fear Him."

One Jewish mother of the period was forced to watch
the torture and murder of her seven sons, but tenderly
encouraged each in his turn to be faithful to God. Their
dying words eloquently illustrate this verse. One said, "Thou
dost dispatch us from this life, but the King of the world
shall raise us up, who have died for His laws, and revive us
to life everlasting." Another extended his limbs for torture
with the words, "These I had from heaven; for His name's
sake I count them naught; from Him I hope to get them
back again." When all the others had died, the youngest son
was offered riches and a position of state if he would deny
God. He answered,

> These brothers, after enduring a brief pain, have now
> drunk of everflowing life, in terms of God's covenant;
> but thou shalt receive by God's judgment the just
> penalty of thine arrogance. I, like my brothers, give
> up body and soul for our fathers' laws, calling on
> God (these deaths are related in II Maccabees 7).

11:36. Others faced the test **of mockings** by many cruel
and sportive tortures. They endured **scourgings** or whip-
pings; they suffered **bonds and imprisonment.** The recipients
of our epistle had endured some trials of faith early in their
Christian lives and had shared with others who were imprisoned for Christ (10:32-34). Jeremiah had know imprisonment for the word of God (Jeremiah 20:2; 37:15; 38:
6), as had Joseph for his faithfulness to God (Genesis 39).

Others includes individuals not yet mentioned, and perhaps unknown to us, but known to the original readers.
The tortures endured by the seven faithful brothers already
mentioned compare in severity and depravity with any
atrocities of times nearer ourselves. The tormentors tore
out the tongue of the oldest brother, scalped and mutilated
him in the presence of his younger brothers and his mother,
then fried his body, maimed but still alive, in a huge cauldron

ings, yea, moreover of bonds and imprisonment:

37 They were stoned, they were sawn asunder, were tempted, were slain with the sword: they wandered about

---

(II Maccabees 7:1-5). The others suffered similar agonies, but we will follow the advice of the final verse in that chapter and "let this suffice" for "the excesses of barbarity."

11:37. Long before Stephen, men of God had been **stoned** to death for their faithfulness. When Joash was king of Judah and the nation turned from God, a prophet named Zechariah came to testify against the people. "And they conspired against him and stoned him with stones at the commandment of the king in the court of the house of the Lord" (II Chronicles 24:17-21).

Tradition has Jeremiah stoned to death by the Jews who took him into Egypt after the captivity of Judah (see Jeremiah 42-44). Nor was he the only man of God to meet this fate from those who were called God's people (Matthew 23:37; II Corinthians 11:25).

Others for their faith **were sawn asunder.** Very ancient Jewish traditions say that Isaiah was killed with a wooden saw under the reign of Manasseh. Scripture does not confirm this story, but one can well imagine such an act from a king who offered his own children in pagan sacrifice (II Chronicles 33:6) and who made the people of Judah "do worse than the heathen" (verse nine).

Faithful saints **were tempted** in many ways, but held fast their confidence in the God they could not see. It has been suggested that the word here translated **tempted** might, by the change of one letter, be translated "met death by fire." This was the fate of some faithful ones during the time of the Maccabees (II Maccabees 6:11), but textual evidence does not appear to warrant such a change here.

Some were **slain with the sword** for their faith, although others by faith escaped this death (verse 34). Elijah was spared when others died (I Kings 19:10). Jeremiah escaped the sword when Urijah was slain (Jeremiah 26:23-24). Herod killed James with the sword but Peter was spared

in sheepskins and goatskins; being destitute, afflicted, tormented;

38 (Of whom the world was not worthy:) they wandered in deserts, and in mountains, and in dens and caves of the earth.

39 And these all, having obtained a good report through faith, received not the promise:

(Acts 12:2ff). Only God knows why some died and others did not, but the faith of each will have its reward.

Because they walked by faith, God's people have sometimes lost their homes and have been forced to **wander about in sheepskins and goatskins.** While it is true that Elijah (II Kings 1:8), John the Baptist (Mark 1:6) and perhaps others (Zechariah 13:4) wore hairy garments, our author speaks of a condition brought on by force, not choice, and apparently intends some others than these.

11:38. Godless crowds have cried that faithful saints were unfit for this world (Acts 22:22). With this our author agrees, though with an opposite meaning! Of such **the world was not worthy,** so they lived in **deserts, mountains, caves** or **dens** while they waited for their heavenly city and eternal homeland.

We see Elijah hiding at Horeb, Elisha at Carmel, or 100 prophets in caves. During the period between the testaments, many of the faithful were forced to forsake their homes to seek safety in remote areas. E. M. Zerr believes the prophecies of Daniel 11:31-36 were fulfilled in the persecutions of that period; Keil includes the Maccabeean heroes but only in a larger picture.

11:39. What was said earlier of the patriarchs (verse 13) is said now of **all these** faithful men and women. They **obtained a good report** or were subjects of good testimony regarding their **faith** — whether directly from God (verse four) or by later men of faith (verse two). Yet they **received not the** particular **promise** which faith always grasps — that final and complete inheritance from the invisible God who is trusted to be a rewarder.

We must not take this to mean that these ancient saints were outside the provisions of divine grace or that they

**40 God having provided some better thing for us, that
they without us should not be made perfect.**

---

will not be among the glorified faithful with Christ in
eternity (see notes on 12:23). Indeed they were justified
by faith — they had this testimony — and the offering of
Christ declares that God was righteous in accepting them
because of their faith (9:15; Romans 3:25-26).

11:40. The fact that their faith was unrewarded in life is
not a sign that faith is ineffective or that God is unfaithful.
It is rather a pointer to the unity of all men of faith in
every dispensation or age. **They** who lived by faith before
Christ were **not perfect** or complete **without** those of **us** who
know God through Christ in the new covenant. "Christ himself is the essential bond of union which binds together the
saints of all ages" (Milligan).

At the same time, **God** has **provided** something **for us**
that is **better** than anything they were given. This is the
knowledge of a high priest who has offered a perfect
sacrifice for sins once for all, who now sits at God's right
hand making intercession for His people, who has opened
the way into heaven by His own life and death, and who
has promised to return to His people to share the glory with
them He has already acquired as their representative.

Better is a key word in Hebrews and is characteristic of
the new covenant with all it offers, particularly in contrast
to the former covenant and institutions. It is used of Christ's
name or position (1:4), His dedicatory sacrifices of the
heavenly sanctuary (9:23), the new testament (7:22) or
covenant (8:6), the Christian hope (7:19), resurrection
(11:35), country (11:16), substance (10:34) and message of
Christ's blood (12:24). It is also used of the behavior these
blessings should elicit from Christ's people (6:9).

The verb **make perfect** is also a frequent one in this
epistle. It is used both of Christ (2:10; 5:9; 7:28) and of
those covered by His sacrifice (7:19; 9:9; 10:14; 12:23).
Such perfection is given through faith: faith that accomplishes great feats, but also faith that suffers and endures.
Perhaps most of all it is the faith that endures. That is our
author's chief point now as he urges the lesson on his
readers.

CHAPTER 12

1 Wherefore seeing we also are compassed about with
so great a cloud of witnesses, let us lay aside every weight,

---

CHAPTER TWELVE

12:1. **Wherefore** here translates a compound Greek
word composed of three lesser particles, each meaning
"therefore" or "wherefore." This very strong combination
word occurs only one other time in the New Testament (I
Thessalonians 4:8). Here the emphasis is in view of the
great cloud of witnesses to whom our author has called
attention in the last chapter and whose presence he now puts
forward as strong inducement for the faithfulness of his
readers.

Cloud frequently stood for a great host in both secular
Greek literature and in the Old Testament (Ezekiel 38:9, 16).
The Greek word translated **witnesses** gives the English word
"martyrs." It first meant one who saw or experienced something, then, one who gave a testimony or bore witness of his
experience. Because one's testimony often led to his persecution or even death, the term gradually came to designate
one whose witness cost him his life. So derives our word
"martyr." The word carried this idea in several biblical
passages although it only later gained this exclusive significance (Nehemiah 9:26; Acts 22:20; Revelation 2:13).

Some of the **witnesses** of chapter eleven were martyrs
in the narrower sense, but they all were witnesses. They had
seen Him who is invisible, and they had seen the realities
of the world of faith. They had given their testimony to these
realities, usually in a hostile environment and to an unbelieving audience. They had been the subject of other
testimony, as God gave them a witness that He was pleased
with their faith.

The term **compassed about** or surrounded, as well as
the clear athletic imagery which follows, suggests that these
individuals are now witnesses in still another sense. "Each
of them has, in his own age and in his own way, run his
section of the great 'relay race,' and, having handed on the
torch to his successor, has joined the multitude of interested

**and the sin which doth so easily beset us, and let us run
with patience the race that is set before us,**

---

spectators and skilled judges" (Robinson). Delitzsch speaks
of "our life here" as "a contest, its theatre the universe, the
seats of the spectators ranged through heaven!" That these
witnesses are spectators of our race must be inferred from
the context; the word itself does not carry that idea.

Because of these faithful saints who encourage **us** by
their record, and perhaps by their own watching, we are
admonished negatively to **lay aside** every hindrance or
distraction, and positively to **run with patience** or endurance
the course which has been laid out for us.

Weight is used in the literature of the time of any ex-
cess poundage, frequently of obesity or stoutness, which the
athlete must shed before he runs. The Christian must put
off all that does not measure up to his calling and is not
becoming to his intentions. The term also suggests the
weights worn by an athlete in training which are then laid
aside for the actual contest.

Sin surrounds the believer to distract him from the
goal. Like the flowing garment worn in the first century,
it also clings to him and impedes his progress. Sin itself, of
every sort and all kinds, must be renounced by the man
running the race of faith. This present context suggests the
particular sin of disbelief which results in apostasy.

It is not enough to begin the race only to fall during
its course. This was the point of Israel's example in chapters three and four, and the thought which triggered the
present discussion in 10:36. The Christian must **run with
patience the race set before** him. The object is not speed but
endurance. The prize is not for the first runner through
but for every runner who finishes.

Paul uses the imagery of the runner in several epistles
(see I Corinthians 9:24-27; Galatians 2:2; Philippians 2:16;
II Timothy 4:7). The terms "fight," "strive," and "conflict"
often represent a single Greek word also taken from the
vocabulary of the athlete or soldier.

Similar language is used in the so-called Fourth Book

    2 Looking unto Jesus the author and finisher of our
faith; who for the joy that was set before him endured
the cross, despising the shame, and is set down at the right

---

of Maccabees, a Jewish writing of uncertain date and
authorship, which credits the victories of Jewish heroes
to the use of proper reason. I quote the following passage
because many readers will not have opportunity to see it
elsewhere. Speaking of his intertestamental heroes the
writer says:

> For truly it was a holy war which was fought by
> them. For on that day virtue, proving them through
> endurance, set before them the prize of victory in
> incorruption in everlasting life. . . . The tyrant was
> their adversary and the world and the life of man
> were the spectators. And righteousness won the vic-
> tory, and gave the crown to her athletes. Who but
> wondered at the athletes of the true Law? (17:11-17).

    12:2. Patience for the course may be found by **looking**
intently and constantly **unto Jesus,** who is not only a witness
of faith but is its **author** or pioneer (the same word used
at 2:10) and its **finisher** or perfecter. Barnes applies these
two expressions to the race official who enrolls entrants and
awards the final prizes, but he gives no support for this
interpretation. More likely the thought is that Jesus (our
author here uses His human name, perhaps to stress His
unity with His people) is **author** of faith because He was the
first to run faith's course all the way to its goal in heaven.
He is **finisher** or perfecter because He leads all who follow
Him to the same finish or end or goal (see I Peter 1:9).

    Jesus has experienced faith's trials and its reward. **The
joy set before him** may refer to His delight in doing the
will of God (Psalm 40:8; Hebrews 10:5-10), but it has special
reference to the promised position of Savior and Lord which
He would be given on behalf of His people (see 2:9; 5:4-10;
Isaiah 53:10-12). Jesus received God's promise in faith.
He placed Himself within the Father's purpose in simple
and wholehearted trust. He then **endured** all that came in
the course of the Father's will with forward-looking faith
and joy and hope.

    The cross was a symbol of great **shame** in the first cen-
tury world. It represented a death reserved for political in-

hand of the throne of God.

3 For consider him that endured such contradiction of sinners against himself, lest ye be wearied and faint in your minds.

4 Ye have not yet resisted unto blood, striving against sin.

---

surrectionists or the basest of criminals. Roman citizens were not only guaranteed immunity from crucifixion (Peter was crucified but Paul was beheaded, according to reliable tradition!) but Cicero urged Romans not to talk about, look at or think on this death. Yet Christ **despised** or considered as insignificant this ignoble suffering when measured against the joy to be had through patient submission to the will of God.

Nor was His faith in vain, for when this epistle was written Christ was already **set down at the right hand of the throne of God.** The verb tense here indicates not only that He had taken this seat but that He still occupies it! For a discussion of the use of Psalm 110 in the New Testament see comments at 1:13; 8:1 and 10:12. Christ led the way in the procession of faith. He has now arrived at faith's goal. He now guarantees the safe passage of all who follow Him in trusting endurance.

12:3. **Consider** this Jesus, our author urges. Do not merely glance at Him, but literally "draw an analogy" between His situation and your own. He **endured** verbal and active **contradition** or opposition from **sinners.** Compare your own sufferings to His so that you do not become **wearied** and **faint** or fall out **in your minds.** The words point again to the race track and the runner who tires to the point of exhaustion.

12:4. In contrast to Jesus, the readers have **not yet resisted unto blood.** Some think this expression alludes to the barehanded boxers of the day who fought until their hands were bleeding and bruised. Your **striving** or fight **against sin** has not reached this point of total dedication, our author would be saying. It is possible, however, to regard the words in the most natural sense and say the original readers of Hebrews had not yet faced the threat of martyr-

5 And ye have forgotten the exhortation which speaketh unto you as unto children, My son, despise not thou the chastening of the Lord, nor faint when thou art rebuked of him:

6 For whom the Lord loveth he chasteneth, and scourgeth every son whom he receiveth.

7 If ye endure chastening, God dealeth with you as with sons; for what son is he whom the father chasteneth not?

---

dom, though some of their predecessors might have (13:7). Jesus followed the way of faith to the cross. His followers must also be willing to die for their faith, if necessary.

12:5-6. In verses five through eleven our writer presents another figure with different imagery. **You have forgotten the exhortation** of Proverbs 3:11-12, he says, in which the believer views his circumstances as discipline from a father who loves his children. Much of the wisdom contained in Proverbs (particularly chapters 1-7) is addressed by the king to his son. The words which follow are taken from that setting and are applied to God's children of the new covenant.

Chastening in this entire context translates a more general word meaning discipline in all its forms. It involves the training of a son by the father. It is the **discipline** or training which makes **disciples**. Such discipline is a sure proof of the father's love (see Revelation 3:19). For this reason its recipients ought not to **despise** or belittle its value and purpose. God first disciplines, then **receives**, His child who has been so molded.

12:7. **If** is only one letter different in the original language from a preposition meaning "for" or "unto," and the better manuscripts and later versions here have the latter. It is for the very kind of discipline or **chastening** described just now that **ye** presently **endure**, the author points out. **God** is simply treating you **as sons**, and sons are disciplined by their fathers. Your suffering is neither without God's knowledge or His purpose. The verb may also be translated as an imperative ("endure for the purpose of discipline"), but it is probably a simple indicative stating what is the case.

8 But if ye be without chastisement, whereof all are partakers, then are ye bastards, and not sons.

9 Furthermore we have had fathers of our flesh which corrected us, and we gave them reverence: shall we not much rather be in subjection unto the Father of spirits, and live?

10 For they verily for a few days chastened us after their own pleasure; but he for our profit, that we might be

---

12:8. If you were **without** any **chastisement** or discipline there would be cause for alarm, for it is the illegitimate son who is unrestrained, untrained, unpunished and sometimes unknown by his father. The son who will bear the father's name with pride in the next generation must bear up under the father's rod now if he is to be fitted for the task. Again our author joins warning to reassurance. "But you **are all partakers** of this discipline and may therefore know you are beloved children" (see 6:9; 10:39).

12:9. Ordinary human experience demonstrates these truths. **We have** all **had** human, fleshly **fathers.** They **corrected** us. We later understood and appreciated that discipline— and even then **we gave** them **reverence** or respect. How **much rather** should **we be in subjection** to our spiritual **father,** whose discipline is part of His grand design to lead us to abiding and true life in communion with Him!

"Fathers of our flesh" is a Hebraic manner of saying "our fleshly fathers." "Father of spirits" is in simple contrast to the other expression, and ought not to be strained to fit either side of the metaphysical argument concerning the origin of individual spirits. Milligan sees a special contrast.

> Our earthly fathers are like ourselves, carnal, frail, sinful mortals . . . liable to err in their discipline. . . . God . . . has none of the weaknesses and infirmities of the flesh . . . [and] can not like our earthly fathers err in His chastisements.

That contrast is clearly made in the next verse.

12:10. During the **few days** of our childhood, our earthly fathers **chastened** or trained us **after their own pleasure.** Sometimes they might have acted hastily or in anger; they

partakers of his holiness.

11 Now no chastening for the present seemeth to be joyous, but grievous: nevertheless afterward it yieldeth the peaceable fruit of righteousness unto them which are exercised thereby.

12 Wherefore lift up the hands which hang down, and the feeble knees;

---

always acted under human limitations of knowledge and design. Our heavenly Father, on the other hand, knows exactly what is needful **for** our **profit** as He prepares us to be **partakers** or sharers **of his holiness.** This holiness involves not only the judicial pronouncement of a new state because of union with Christ (10:10, 14, 29), but also a daily life of godly thinking and behavior (see verse 14).

12:11. One writer remarked of this verse that "the only proper commentary is our own personal experience." All discipline, however instructive, is painful at the time it is administered, but later its benefits are seen in those who appropriate the intended training. **The peaceable fruit** of such training is **righteousness.** Peace and righteousness are related in both the Old (Isaiah 32:17) and the New Testaments (James 3:18). Here the fruit is **peaceable** in contrast to the discipline which produced it.

12:12. In this verse and the next our author quotes from Isaiah 35:3 and the Greek version of Proverbs 4:26. He changes imagery to that of a group of wayfarers on a journey, and builds on this figure through verse 17.

Lift up the weary travellers' **hands which hang down** slack and loose from exhaustion; lend strength to **the feeble knees** which have lost their power to hold up and have become as paralyzed. These were appropriate exhortations as addressed to Jews who would return to their homeland from faraway Persia. (The journey theme is also seen in Isaiah 40:3-4, 29-31; 43:2, 5-7, 19-21; 48:20-21; 49:8-13; 52: 10-11; 58:11-12). The same exhortations are appropriately given to faith-pilgrims of the new covenant who have become weary in well doing and are about to faint with fatigue. It should also be noticed that this encouragement is given to believers as a company, and that their pilgrimage involves

**13 And make straight paths for your feet, lest that
which is lame be turned out of the way; but let it rather be
healed.**

---

mutual concern and careful attention to one another (see
comments at 3:12-13; 9:17; 10:24).

12:13. As believers travel together toward the heavenly
city, they are to **make straight paths** so that the **feet** of those
who are **lame** will not **be turned out of the way.** The latter
phrase has been translated two ways. The reading of the
King James Version agrees with the thought of the Greek
text of Proverbs 4:26-27, which urges making straight paths,
then says not to turn to the right hand or to the left. Many
other versions translate our author equally well with a slightly different thought as "lest the lame limb be dislocated altogether," or words to that effect. This translation more
obviously contrasts with the next statement of this verse,
but let it rather be healed.

Either phrasing is possible from the Greek and both
thoughts are appropriate. Let the Christian pilgrim remove
from the path anything that would impede the progress
of his weak brethren or cause them to stumble. Let nothing
be left before them which would cause one to miss the trail
or would trip a lame traveller and put his limbs completely
out of joint. Rather let each sojourner bear with his fellows,
lend them strength when needed, help with the burdens of
the weak, encourage the faint-hearted and clear the path for
those who are tired and weak.

The verb form of the word here translated **lame** is used
in I Kings 18:21 (Greek translation) of those Israelities
who were "halting between two opinions" and could not de-
cide whether to serve Jehovah or Baal. This passage suggests at least one form of lameness which afflicted the weak
Hebrew saints who first received this epistle. They were
weak in the faith. They were wobbling between allegiance to
Jesus Christ and to their former Jewish religion. The term
should not be limited to this application though it seems
to include it.

14 Follow peace with all men, and holiness, without
which no man shall see the Lord:

15 Looking diligently lest any man fail of the grace of

12:14. In their journey together it is essential that the
travellers **follow** or actively seek **peace with all** their companions. The phrase is from Psalm 34:14. Peter quotes it also
in his letter which, interesting enough, is addressed "to
those who reside as aliens" (I Peter 3:11; 1:1, New American
Standard Bible).

Such scriptural injunctions to peace or love need not
be followed by immediate explanations which practically
annul the biblical point. It is a pitiable generation in which
the church is so strife-infested that peace and love are
held as unholy words in some quarters. Many church quar-
rels have been blamed on error or attributed to truth which
actually resulted from carnal and fleshly minds. The fault
has often been with some who refused to put others ahead
of self, to bear patiently with the weak, to seek peace at
the expense of personal pride or opinions. It has sometimes
been, in short, with those who simply refused to obey
the clear teaching of the Word of God. It is one thing
to stand for clear truth against clear error. It is quite another to call all one's own thoughts and inferences "truth,"
then immediately draw the circle of peace closely about
those personal conclusions.

Those following Jesus in the highway of faith must
seek **holiness** as well as peace, for **without** holiness **no man
shall see the Lord**. Only the pure in heart will see God
(Matthew 5:8). Holiness has always been required of God's
people, and the command has always been grounded in
the character of God who gave it (Leviticus 11:45; I Peter
1:15-16). If peace makes association possible with brethren,
holiness makes it possible with God.

12:15. **Looking diligently** translates a Greek word from
which comes our "overseer" or "bishop." It is "as if they
were travelling together on some long journey, in a large
company, and he says, 'Take heed that no man be left behind; I do not seek this only, that ye may arrive yourselves,
but also that ye should look diligently after the others'"
(Chrysostom). It is the duty of the experienced (elder)

God; lest any root of bitterness springing up trouble you, and thereby many be defiled;

Christian shepherds (pastors) to look carefully to the spiritual needs of their flock as overseers (bishops), and this responsibility is laid directly upon them by the Holy Spirit. As the same time, every pilgrim of faith has a similar duty to his fellow-wayfarers, and that is the point of this verse.

A congregation of saints will never enjoy the blessings of brotherhood and Christian love that God provides and intends so long as it conceives of itself primarily in institutional or external terms. The Christian religion is a religion of togetherness: saints together constitute the family of God in each place. They are to love as brethren. It is so difficult for men today to pass beyond the carnal view of the church, as a sort of religious club or organization, to its true nature as revealed in the Bible. This view must be seen if saints are ever to comprehend the real beauty of their actual state together in Christ.

Look diligently so that no one **fail** or come short of (see also 4:1) **the grace of God** that is given freely in Christ and enjoyed by faith. The figure here is that of the traveller who lags behind and never reaches the end of the journey. It is a sin of too many churches that saints may wander in one day and out the next with very little notice given either to their presence or absence. God's words concerning His Old Testament church often describe His New Testament people as well: "My sheep wandered through all the mountains, and upon every high hill; yea, my flock was scattered upon all the face of the earth, and none did search or seek after them" (Ezekiel 34:6).

Still using the pilgrimage motif, our author warns against **any root of bitterness**, or poisonous root, which might be cut as for food and result in widespread contamination of the people. The term comes from Deuteronomy 29:18, where Moses uses it figuratively to warn Israel against turning from God to idols. Our author has already spoken against an evil heart of unbelief which leads one from the living God (3:12). Here he repeats the warning in figurative terms.

16 Lest there be any fornicator, or profane person, as Esau, who for one morsel of meat sold his birthright.

17 For ye know how that afterward, when he would have inherited the blessing, he was rejected: for he found

---

12:16. Watch diligently for any fornicator, not in the limited usage of the word alone, but as signifying any moral uncleanness. Some interpret this warning as against spiritual adultery, and equate it with turning from God. Our writer warns against sexual impurity, however, in 13:4, and it is preferable to take the warning literally here.

The profane person is one who has no regard for what is holy. He is unable — or worse, unwilling — to distinguish between what is common and what is holy. Such an attitude frequently leads to immorality as well as other sins.

Esau is given as an example of a profane man. Jewish tradition made him a fornicator as well. For one morsel of meat or food he sold his birthright (Genesis 25:29-34). "The rights of primogeniture were among the most noble, honorable, and spiritual in the ancient world" (Barnes). Esau not only "despised" his double portion of the inheritance, he scoffed at his role in the patriarchal line through which God's covenant promises and election purposes were to be fulfilled. Behind many particular sins lies a basic inability to distinguish between what is valuable and what is of little importance. Christians who fail to appreciate their position in the Lord Jesus Christ are often prone to grievous sins. The best preventive against sin is a constant awareness of who and what one is called and called to be in the Son of God, and a regular meditation on one's position as he stands identified with the blameless Son before the Father.

12:17. The consequences of profanity involve not only the present loss of blessing but also the future impossibility of renewal. The disregard for what is holy, which leads to sin in the first place, also prevents true repentance — even when the profane man sees his final end and is overcome with remorse. Esau also illustrates this fact (see comments at 10:26-29).

Ye know from the Old Testament story how that afterward when Esau desired to inherit the blessing he was re-

no place of repentance, though he sought it carefully with tears.

18 For ye are not come unto the mount that might be touched, and that burned with fire, nor unto blackness, and

---

jected (Genesis 27:30-40). Three phrases in this verse are subject to more than one interpretation. Was Esau **rejected** by Isaac, by God, or by both? Did Esau find **no place of repentance** in himself or in his father or in both? Did **he** seek **carefully with tears** the blessing, or a place for repentance?

Esau's rejection may safely be said to have been by both God and Isaac, since the patriarchal blessing was ultimately given by God through the father (see comment at 11:20). When Isaac affirmed the certainty of Jacob's blessing, he was pointing out its divine origin (Genesis 27:33).

Esau found no **place** for **repentance** because there was no change of his father's mind regarding the blessing already given. Delitzsch sees Esau as "a type of the hopelessly apostate" and argues that he did not experience true repentance himself at all, but simply changed his mind about the inheritance and blessing when he realized the point to which his careless attitude had led. **Repentance** here has its most basic meaning of a change of mind, but it involves a change of mind that seeks to change the effects of the previous disposition. Esau could not find such a change of mind in his father Isaac, nor was he able to change the effects of his own former attitude (whether or not he had the same attitude still).

Esau **sought** the blessing **with tears** (Genesis 27:38), but this involved tears for his father's change of mind. Both alternatives ought here to be included.

12:18. Again the imagery changes, this time to terms based on the giving of the Law at Sinai. **Ye who follow Jesus,** the enthroned Son at the Father's right hand, **are not come to** a mountain such as Sinai. There ancient Israel had gathered as God's elect nation, to receive the details and requirements of the covenant which graciously bound them to Him. According to the accounts of Exodus (19:16, 18) and Deuteronomy (4:11; 5:23; 9:15), the top of Sinai **burned with fire.**

darkness, and tempest,

19 And the sound of a trumpet, and the voice of words; which voice they that heard entreated that the word should not be spoken to them any more:

20 (For they could not endure that which was commanded, And if so much as a beast touch the mountain, it shall be stoned, or thrust through with a dart:

21 And so terrible was the sight, that Moses said, I exceedingly fear and quake:)

The lower parts of the mountain were hidden by the **blackness** and **darkness** of the storm clouds which covered them. Out of the clouds came loud noises and bursts of fierce storm and **tempest**.

12:19. When the people heard a **sound** as of a **trumpet** (Exodus 19:16-19) and **the voice of words** from God (Deuteronomy 5:22), they **entreated that the word should not be spoken to them any more** directly, but rather through the mediation of Moses (Exodus 20:18-19; Deuteronomy 5:23-27).

12:20. The assembly of Israel was awed and terror-stricken by the thought of God's command (Exodus 19:12-13) that **if so much as a beast touch the mountain, it shall be stoned**. The phrase **thrust through with a dart** is not in the better manuscripts or in most later versions. The Old Testament command has the animal stoned (apparently if it wanders off the mountain within distance of the people) or shot (with an arrow, if it remains on the mountain out of the people's reach).

12:21. Even **Moses** was so overcome by the **terrible** or terror-inspiring **sight** as to remark, **I exceedingly fear and quake**. This statement is not reported in the Old Testament, though it is in keeping with what is stated there. Exodus 19:19 says that when the trumpet sound became louder and louder "Moses spake, and God answered him by a voice." What Moses said is not told. The Greek text of Exodus 19:18 says that all the people were driven out of their senses for fear, and Moses would certainly be included in that statement. Whether our author depends on that text or some other source for his information we do not know. What he writes, however, is Scripture, and as such has the absolute approval and endorsement of the Holy Spirit.

22 But ye are come unto mount Zion, and unto the city of the living God, the heavenly Jerusalem, and to an innumerable company of angels,

---

12:22. As fearful and terrifying as that scene was, the new-covenant saint has aproached God under circumstances and in company far more demanding of a faithful response.

The word translated **ye are come** (here and at verse 18) in its noun form gives the English word "proselyte," suggestive perhaps of the move of the Hebrews from Judaism to Christ. All Christians, however, have come at conversion, and remain throughout life, in the presence of the figures and elements which follow.

Mount Zion is literally Zion-mountain, in contrast to Sinai-mountain. Zion was first a Jebusite stronghold in the Old Testament, but David captured it with his private army and made it his capital of united Israel (II Samuel 5:6-9). Since it had not formerly been a part of Judah or Israel, Zion was politically independent, much as Washington, D.C. in the United States. David brought the Ark of the Covenant to Zion in the next chapter. God's approval is seen in the dynastic and messianic promises given to David through the prophet Nathan (II Samuel 7; see I Kings 14:21; Psalm 78: 68).

Solomon's Temple was actually on Mount Moriah, but the term **Zion** came to include that as well. In the Psalms, Zion is frequently celebrated as the holy city of God's choosing and the meeting place of His people Israel (see 120-134, especially 132-134).

The reference here is not to physical Zion, but to its heavenly prototype, which is part of **the city of the living God.** Our author has spoken already of this city (11:10, 14-16). He mentions it again in 13:14. We have not come to an earthly city, but to the **heavenly Jerusalem** where God dwells in glory.

A glorified Jerusalem was the subject of much Jewish speculation (between the testaments, including material from the Dead Sea Scrolls) and of some revelation (the very difficult chapters 40-48 of Ezekiel). The author of Hebrews adds to inspired knowledge on the topic, as do

23 To the general assembly and church of the firstborn, which are written in heaven, and to God the Judge of
all, and to the spirits of just men made perfect,

Paul and John (see references and comments at 11:10).
That is not to say that all these biblical passages apply to
the same things in every detail; each must be studied in its
own context for the specific meaning. This verse clearly refers to the place where God dwells, to which Christ has
opened the way by passing through the veil in His flesh,
and to which Christians have come in their new-covenant
faith in Him.

Included in this same awe-inspiring scene are an
innumerable company, literally tens of thousands or myraids,
of angels (see Psalm 68:17; Daniel 7:10; Revelation 5:11).
These angels are sent forth by God for the service of His
saints on earth (1:14), but in all their activities they exist
for the praise of God.

12:23. **The general assembly** translates a word which
gives the English "panegyric." This Greek term is used in
Greek literature of a public festival or celebration attended
by all the people. Such celebrations usually included the
praise of great men. There is some controversy as to whether
the festive assembly here includes only the angels or also
those mentioned next.

Church should be interpreted in its literal sense here of
an assembly. It is composed of **the firstborn** ones (plural in
the original) who **are written** or enrolled as citizens **in** the
city of God in **heaven.** The phrase has been taken as of the
angels or of first-generation Christians, but it seems best to
think of **the church of the firstborn** ones as being the church
of Christ of all times and all places on earth. As firstborn
ones, Christians must heed the warning against profaneness
already given concerning Esau, another firstborn (verses
16-17).

God, the Judge of all, is present, and He will acquit or
condemn each man. Here is a word of comfort for a suffering church, for God's judgments will involve a vindication
of its cause (see comments at 10:30-31). That the presence
of God speaks of comfort and not fear for His people is
seen in the phrase that follows.

**24   And to Jesus the mediator of the new covenant,
and to the blood of sprinkling, that speaketh better things
than that of Abel.**

The spirits of just men made perfect refers to those
saints who lived and died before Christ but who walked according to faith during their lives. They are declared **just**
because the Judge has viewed their faith and pronounced
them so on the basis of Christ's atonement (9:15). They
are now **made perfect** or complete because they have arrived
at the state of blessed rest with the Lord which was publicly announced with the beginning of the gospel proclama-
tion. And the gospel speaks essentially of the life, death and
resurrection of the eternal Son who partook of flesh and
blood, but now sits as eternal Priest-King at the right hand
of God. Just as the ancient saints could not be made perfect
without their new-covenant counterparts (11:40), so we must
live in view of them (see comments at 12:1).

12:24. **Jesus, the mediator of the new covenant** is present (see 8:6). **Jesus** is His saving name and associates Him
with His earthly brethren (Matthew 1:21; Hebrews 2:9-18).
New here means "recent," and refers to the nearness in time
between these first readers and the covenant Jesus had
inaugurated shortly before. The presence of Jesus speaks
assurance, for He is surety of the new-covenant promises
(see comments at 7:22, 25; also Appendix IV on Christ's
Sacrifice and the Christian).

The blood of sprinkling is the blood of Christ. Our writer has already spoken of sprinkled blood in terms of purification (9:13-14; 10:22), of covenant-ratification (9:19), and
of Passover (11:28). Each figure bespeaks blessings for
those bound to the Son who has now shed His blood on their
behalf.

Christ's blood **speaks better** or more powerfully than the
blood associated with **Abel,** whether one thinks of Abel's own
blood shed by Cain or the sacrificial blood he shed by faith.
Christ's blood also speaks **of** better things than either blood,
for Abel's sacrifice spoke of atonement hoped-for, and his
own blood called for vengeance. Christ's blood, however,
assures all martyrs of faith that their blood was not shed in

25 See that ye refuse not him that speaketh. For if

---

vain, and it speaks of an atonement which Christ has already
accomplished and the Father has already accepted.

The two covenants are contrasted in this manner. The
first began at fearful Mount Sinai, a mountain characterized
by warnings and threats. The second began with glorious
Mount Zion, populated by servant angels and saved men
praising a holy God and His priestly Son. The first description closed with a voice of words which sent the people
scurrying and left even Moses trembling. The second description closed with a Mediator's blood which speaks with elo-
quence and power of an accomplished atonement and the
reward of faithfulness.

The exhortation to steadfastness in the midst of affliction is now coming to an end. Our author has demonstrated
himself in this chapter to be a user as well as an author
of Scripture. His exhortation here is built around four
figures. First is the spiritual athlete, striving for the prize.
He is encouraged by the former contestants who now watch,
but especially by Jesus who is both author and finisher
of faith. Second is the child, who meekly learns from the pur-
poseful discipline of his loving father. Third is the company of pilgrims, who watch for one another as they move
toward their destination. Fourth is the contrast between
the Old Testament and New Testament churches, as gathered
respectively before their covenant God.

The first illustration called on chapter eleven, which itself drew from the entire Old Testament and intertestamental
periods. The second illustration came from Proverbs, representing the Writings portion of the Hebrew Old Testament.
The third was based on Isaiah, though it drew from other
parts of Scripture as well. It stood for the Prophets. The
fourth came from Exodus and Deuteronomy, standing for
the books of Moses, the Torah.

In the final five verses of the chapter, our author looks
again to the prophetic portion of his Scriptures, there finding words for his closing appeal.

12:25. **See** or take heed **that** you do **not refuse** God who
is speaking. The thought is directly related to the epistle's

they escaped not who refused him that spake on earth, much more shall not we escape, if we turn away from him that speaketh from heaven:

26 Whose voice then shook the earth: but now he hath promised, saying, Yet once more I shake not the earth only, but also heaven.

27 And this word, Yet once more, signifieth the removing of those things that are shaken, as of things that are made, that those things which cannot be shaken may remain.

---

opening affirmation that God has spoken (1:1-2). How He has spoken and what He has said have been our author's themes throughout. Now He urges care lest the readers fail to respond to the final message in the Son.

They who refused him that spake on earth refers to Israel. They heard God's voice from the smoking mountain (verses 18-21) but failed to heed it and were destroyed (3:8-4:11). If here expresses certainty, not indefiniteness; "since" would be a proper translation. Since their judgment was so sure, though pertaining to an earth-given revelation, punishment is **much more** certain for those who **turn away** from God now that He has spoken **from heaven.** See the opening comments on chapter two for a discussion of this type of argument and other references where it is used.

12:26. When God spoke from Sinai, His **voice shook the earth** (Exodus 19:18; Psalm 18:7; 68:8; 114:4). **But we now** have His promise that **yet once more** He will **shake not the earth only, but also heaven.** The promise is found in Haggai 2:6, and was given by Haggai the prophet to Zerubbabel the governor and Joshua the high priest at the dedication of the rebuilt Temple in 516 B. C. Our author applies the words to the final Day of the Lord (see comments at 10:25).

12:27. The words **yet once more,** our author explains, denote **the removing of those things that are shaken.** For if God will shake the earth **once** more, and apparently only **once** more, that shaking must come at the final shaking of the earth which will also be its **removing.** This is to be expected, he adds, for these are **things that are made,** and

28   Wherefore we receiving a kingdom which cannot be moved, let us have grace, whereby we may serve God acceptably with reverence and godly fear:

29   For our God is a consuming fire.

---

they are by nature temporary (see 1:10-12). Further, it is necessary that those things be shaken and removed, so that those things of the invisible and eternal order which cannot be shaken may remain. It might not be straining the point to say that the trembling of Sinai was an indication that the order it represented would one day pass away, just as the passing glory of Moses' face on that occasion is said to indicate the same thing (II Corinthians 3:7-14).

12:28. Our covenant is based on a word from heaven, however, and is an administration of the eternal and heavenly realities (8:1, 2, 5; 9:1, 11, 24). We have, in fact, received a kingdom which cannot be moved or shaken or ever destroyed. It is the everlasting kingdom of prophecy (Daniel 7:27). We ought, therefore, to have grace (a regular Greek expression for giving thanks), through which we may serve God acceptably with reverence or pious respect and godly fear.

12:29. Such reverence and respectful fear is absolutely required in view of the fact that our God is a consuming fire. The phrase comes from Deuteronomy 4:24 (see that context), but the thought is found in numerous passages (see a partial listing in comments on 10:27).

> It is an aspect of the character of God as revealed in the Bible that plays little part in much present-day thinking about Him; but if we are to be completely "honest to God," we dare not ignore it. Reverence and awe before His holiness are not incompatible with grateful trust and love in response to His mercy (Bruce).

A study of the Bible reveals that those men in each age who were closest to God and enjoyed the most intimate fellowship with Him have been also the most awed by His holiness. One thinks immediately of Abraham, Moses, Isaiah, Paul or the Apostle John. The greatest example is our Lord, who on occasion used the intimate term "Abba," but who more frequently is recorded as addressing God as "Holy Father" or "Righteous Father." Boldness is not audacity.

CHAPTER 13

1 Let brotherly love continue.

"God is love" must always be joined to "our God is a consuming fire," for holy love demands a fire of judgment,
and that fire is holy which consumes the adversaries of God
and His people.

CHAPTER THIRTEEN

Our author has developed his case in twelve chapters.
He has broken into his discussion periodically with urgent
exhortations or earnest warnings. Now he has come to the
end of his literary task, and he closes with specific words of
practical import. Throughout the epistle he has spoken of
God's new-covenant people who have come into a relationship with Him based on the saving work of the Son. The
admonitions of chapter thirteen are addressed to Christians
as faith-pilgrims. Because they share the benefits of Christ's
work, they must encourage and tolerate and forgive each
other.

Some critics have argued that this chapter was not an
original part of Hebrews. They say it has no relation to the
rest of the epistle, and that it was added by a later scribe
or editor. Filson has clearly demonstrated the unity between
this chapter and the previous twelve (see his book listed
in the bibliography). In fact, he affirms that it is this final
chapter which provides a key to the rest of the book. One
does not have to agree with all Filson's conclusions to appreciate his basic point. It is enough here to say that the unity
of Hebrews has been demonstrated convincingly, even from
the standpoint of modern critical scholarship.

13:1. **Brotherly love** properly exists between those shar-
ing a common father (see 2:11). It is more than sentiment or
affection; it involves the practical demonstration of what
is in the heart and mind. The Hebrew Christians had manifested brotherly love soon after their conversion (10:32-34)
and throughout their Christian lives (6:10). Our author does
not tell them to begin its practice, therefore, but to **let** it
continue.

2 Be not forgetful to entertain strangers: for thereby some have entertained angels unawares.

3 Remember them that are in bonds, as bound with them; and them which suffer adversity, as being yourselves also in the body.

13:2. Nor are they to forget hospitality. The Greek word translated **hospitality** literally means a love of strangers or travellers, and the King James Version tries to give this sense in its **entertain strangers**. Inns were available to travellers of the first century, but they were notoriously ill-kept, usually expensive, frequently bawdy and sometimes dangerous.

For these reasons, Jews and Christians normally cared for their own brethren who might be traveling or visiting in a strange city. Paul mentions this practice several times in his epistles. John speaks of the custom and corrects two abuses: that of giving fraternal hospitality and blessing to antichrists who denied the Christian gospel (II John 6-11), and that of failing to extend care to worthy brethren who needed it (III John 5-10). Peter also urges hospitality (I Peter 4:9), which for Christians was grounded in the words of Christ Himself (Matthew 25:35-36). In a book known as the Didache, an unknown Christian who lived shortly after the time of the apostles gave detailed instructions concerning the reception and treatment of traveling preachers and teachers. Later a Roman writer named Lucian called Christians gullible, saying that any tramp could find food and housing if he could convince them of his religion.

Our author notes that **some** in the past **have entertained angels** without knowing it, referring no doubt to Abraham (Genesis 18) and Lot (Genesis 19), and perhaps others. Because of what our author has already stated in 1:14, we must agree with Delitzsch that "any man whom we entertain without knowing any details as to him, may be even for us a very angel of God." Not that this is the general rule, but hospitality does frequently return unexpected blessings, and by it Christ is served.

13:3. The original readers knew what it meant to **remember them in bonds** (10:34), **as bound with them,** and **them which suffer adversity** or literally "have it bad," **as being also in the body.** It is inviting to take the phrases **as**

4 Marriage is honorable in all, and the bed undefiled: but whoremongers and adulterers God will judge.

5 Let your conversation be without covetousness; and

---

bound with them and as being in the body in the sense of
the bond of love (Colossians 3:14) and the body of Christ
(I Corinthians 12). Unless one assumes that Paul wrote
Hebrews, however, he may not be sure that meaning is intended here. Even so, the point of the exhortation is about
the same. Christians are to be so captivated by brotherly
love that when one is bound the others sympathize as being
themselves bound. When some are in bad circumstances the
rest are concerned to help, being subject also to the ailments
of mortality.

13:4. The original text has no verb here and the statement may be translated either as an indicative (as in the
King James Version) or, perhaps better in this context, as
an imperative. Let **marriage** be respected and regarded as
honorable. Let it be free from the sanctions and regulations
of asceticism on the one hand, and the profligate and licen-
tious behavior of libertinism on the other. **In all** may be
interpreted as among all people or in all things. The Greek
expression frequently means simply "altogether" or "completely."

Let **the** marriage **bed** and the relationship it stands for
be **undefiled,** for **God** (this word is emphatic in the original)
will judge the impure (uncleanness, fornication and prostitute are all of the same word-family with this in the Greek)
and **adulterers.** When Scripture makes a distinction between
fornication and adultery the former refers to sexual impurity
in general and in terms of moral uncleanness, while the
latter refers to extramarital sexual relations by a husband
or wife and in terms of the marriage covenant and relationship. A proper respect for the institution and relationship of marriage is the best prevention against God's judgment for fornication or adultery.

13:5. Again the verb must be supplied to urge that the
conversation or turn of mind and life be **without covetousness.** Again there is a verbal link with what has gone before.
Covetousness is literally a love of silver. Our author has

be content with such things as ye have: for he hath said,
I will never leave thee, nor forsake thee.

6 So that we may boldly say, The Lord is my helper,
and I will not fear what man shall do unto me.

7 Remember them which have the rule over you, who
have spoken unto you the word of God: whose faith follow,
considering the end of their conversation:

---

urged love of brethren and love of strangers, but now he
cautions against the love of money. Since this sin comes
from the mind the solution must begin there as well.

Be content with such things as ye have. Milligan ac-
curately states the teaching of Scripture in saying: "Be dili-
gent in business; do all that you can lawfully and consistent-
ly to improve your own condition and to promote the hap-
piness of others; and then with calmness and resignation
leave all the consequences to God."

The basis of such trustful contentment is the word of
God in such passages as Genesis 28:15; Deuteronomy 31:6, 8;
Joshua 1:5; I Chronicles 28:20; Isaiah 41:17; Matthew 6:25-30
and many others, that **I will never leave thee nor forsake
thee.** This promise is made very emphatic in the original
Greek by the succession of three negatives.

13:6. Because God has given His word (and the phrase
quoted here seems to have been common in Jewish speech, to
judge from its use by the non-biblical writer Philo), the believer is to respond with a word of his own. **We may boldly
say** in the words of Psalm 118:6, which were also regularly
quoted during the great feasts of the Jews, **the Lord is my
helper, and I will not fear what man shall do unto me.** Both
the Hebrew and the Greek may also be translated: "The Lord
is my helper and I will not fear. What shall man do unto
me?" In either case, the thought is the same. Because God
speaks in promise the possessor of faith should speak in
trust and confidence.

13:7. As examples of **faith,** the readers should remember their former leaders who used to speak **the word of
God** unto them. Their **conversation** or way of life (not the
same word used in verse five) led them to a praiseworthy
end, which the readers are to be **considering** by thorough

8   Jesus Christ the same yesterday, and today, and for ever.

---

and continuing contemplation. Whether this refers to death by martyrdom or simply a life ending in faith we can not tell. The point is that the faith of these leaders was not in vain. Both the author and his readers had heard the gospel from the apostles (2:3-4). Since we do not know the author, the readers, or even their location, we can not know the specific identity of these who had **the rule** or leadership in earlier days.

13:8. The first leaders had died, but their faithfulness had been consistent. The object of their faith also remains the same. **Jesus Christ the same yesterday, and today, and for ever.** Our author spoke of the eternal "sameness" of Christ in 1:12, quoting from Psalm 102:27. Christ is the greatest example of faithfulness and steadfastness: the same yesterday and today and for ever. He is the same subject of preaching: yesterday, today and for ever. He is the same object of faith: yesterday, today and for ever.

Yesterday seems to refer to our author's immediate past. That was the time when Jesus became lower than the angels, became partaker of flesh and blood, received a body in which to do the will of God, offered Himself as a sinless sacrifice and was subsequently raised from the dead and taken up into glory. **Today** would refer to our author's present. **For ever** would refer to his future.

The atoning work of Christ took place in time and in human history, but that work has now reached its goal. God's salvation-purpose unfolded gradually. With the events involving Christ, which culminated in His position at God's right hand, the earthly work of atonement has reached perfection. No opportunity remains for possible failure, so far as Christ is concerned. He was tempted in all points during His "once for all" ministry, but that took place in the beginning of these last days and will never be repeated. The constant believer in any age may know that his salvation is secured in the person of the Son — the Son at God's right hand in heaven — Jesus Christ, the same yesterday, and today and for ever.

9 Be not carried about with divers and strange doctrines. For it is a good thing that the heart be established with grace; not with meats, which have not profited them that have been occupied therein.

13:9. If the readers will hold fast to the non-changing Christ (verse eight), imitating the faith of their leaders who also trusted in Him (verse seven), they will not **be carried about** as in a flood **with** various **doctrines** or teachings. These teachings are not part of the old familiar gospel or the teachings which had come from the apostles and prophets. Instead they are **strange**, alien and foreign. Specifically, the author warns against teachings about **meats** or foods, **which have not profited** those **occupied** with them, and which draw attention from **grace** by which the **heart** is **established** and strengthened.

At least five explanations have been offered of these teachings about **meats.** (1) Some think of a Jewish dispute over kosher food, over clean and unclean meats, as apparently is the case in 9:10. (2) Others think of meats offered to pagan gentile idols, as in I Corinthians 8. (3) Some suppose he refers to ascetic regulations of a gentile philosophy, as in Colossians. (4) Still others think of sacrificial meats of the Old Testament system, of which some were eaten by the priests and/or the people. (5) And some have suggested a kind of Jewish fellowship meal, as described, for instance, by Josephus.

The entire context of Hebrews seems to narrow the choice to a Jewish answer. The fellowship meal is not attested in Scripture and might not have been a widespread custom at all. Disputes over clean and unclean foods would fit the general context but not these specific verses. The verses following seem to indicate sacrificial meats which were eaten by worshippers and/or the priest who offered them. If such sacrificial meats are intended, the point is that the Christian's sacrifice results in the distribution of grace which strengthens his heart, not in meat which strengthens his body.

13:10. The pagans frequently called Christians atheists because they had no visible gods. It is likely that the Jews pointed to the absence of visible sacrifices and cultic priests

**10 We have an altar, whereof they have no right to
eat which serve the tabernacle.**

**11 For the bodies of those beasts, whose blood is
brought into the sanctuary by the high priest for sin, are
burned without the camp.**

**12 Wherefore Jesus also, that he might sanctify the
people with his own blood, suffered without the gate.**

---

in their attacks on Christians. Our author has already affirmed that Christians have a high priest, though He is in
heaven (8:1). Here he says **we have an altar** as well, and of
its benefits those Jewish priests who used to **serve the Mosaic
tabernacle** do not **have** a **right to** partake or **eat.** An Old
Testament reason is given for this in the next verse.

Some Catholic writers apply this reference to the Mass,
but against such a view stands the once-for-all nature of
Christ's sacrifice in Hebrews, as well as the specific point of
the next verse. Various other authors have explained the
altar as being the cross, or a heavenly altar, or the death of
Christ. It may be best not to seek a specific application, leaving our author's single point to stand alone. Christians do
have an altar and, by metonymy, a sacrifice for their sins.
On that, also see Appendices II and III.

13:11. Under the Old Testament system, when **blood** of
sacrificial animals was **brought into the** most holy place **by
the high priest** as an offering **for sin,** the **bodies of those
beasts** were **burned** outside **the** camp. This was true in general (Leviticus 6:30), and of the Day of Atonement sin-offerings in particular (Leviticus 16:27). Because the offering
of Christ fulfills the sin-offering of the Day of Atonement,
and because it is the only sin-offering God now accepts,
our altar is one of which no Old Testament priest could partake, even according to his own Law!

13:12. In keeping with this figure, **Jesus also suffered**
outside **the gate** of Jerusalem and therefore outside the camp
of Israel, so **that he might sanctify the people with his own
blood.** He not only was treated shamefully (12:2), but He
was in the literal sense an outcast.

13 Let us go forth therefore unto him without the camp, bearing his reproach.

14 For here have we no continuing city, but we seek one to come.

15 By him therefore let us offer the sacrifice of praise to God continually, that is, the fruit of our lips giving thanks to his name.

16 But to do good and to communicate forget not: for with such sacrifices God is well pleased.

13:13. The believer in Christ is to be willing **therefore to go forth unto him** outside **the camp** and fellowship of Israel. If this means **bearing** a **reproach,** the reproach is **his** (see 11:26). To be with Jesus the believer must leave the camp and go outside the gate, for that is where He went. The reproach is overshadowed, however, by the fact that Jesus' death not only was that of a sin-offering, but was the only sin-offering God will ever again accept.

13:14. The loss of fellowship in the city of the Jews is further softened by the fact that Christ's people are faith-pilgrims who **seek** another city which is yet **to come,** though they have already come to it by faith (see comments at 12:22-24). On the other hand, the **city** which is **here** on earth (Jerusalem) is **no continuing city** at all, and either had been or shortly would be destroyed when our author wrote this epistle.

13:15. **By** Christ, the high priest and mediator, Christians are urged to **offer** their **sacrifice to God continually** (see 7:25). This is not a sin-offering. Only Christ offers that, and He offered one sacrifice one time for all men of all time. The believer offers a **sacrifice of praise,** the same term used in the Greek Old Testament for the peace-offering of thanksgiving (Leviticus 7:12-25). **The fruit of lips giving thanks to his name** did not originate with the new covenant (Psalm 50:12-15, 23; 141:2; Hosea 14:2). Such praise does belong to it, however, and fulfills the types of thank-offerings under the old covenant.

13:16. **God** is also **well pleased with** the spiritual **sacrifices** offered by His people when they do **not forget to do good, and to communicate** or to share with those in need

17 Obey them that have the rule over you, and submit yourselves: for they watch for your souls, as they that must give account, that they may do it with joy, and not with grief: for that is unprofitable for you.

18 Pray for us: for we trust we have a good conscience, in all things willing to live honestly.

(Amos 5:21-24; Micah 6:6-12). **Communicate** translates the verb of the "fellowship" family.

13:17. The practical instructions continue, this time with regard to Christian leaders or **them that have the rule.** The community of faith is to **obey them** because of persuasion and to **submit** to their guidance. The leaders, on the other hand, have a charge to **watch for** the **souls** of those in the community, for whom **they must give account.** If Christians do submit and obey as the rulers watch and lead, the report **may be with joy and not with grief,** which would be **unprofitable** for those of whom a bad account was given.

Dods relates **that** which is **unprofitable** to the **watch for your souls** rather than the **give account,** and suggests that believers are to obey and submit so that the watching by the leaders will be a joyful task. A failure to cooperate will not only cause grief to those watching, but will make their work unprofitable for those for whose sake it is done.

The figure of a watchman comes from the Old Testament, particularly from Ezekiel (3:17-21; 33:1-9). Here it is joined to the pastoral task of the spiritual shepherd. While the leaders in this chapter are given no technical or descriptive name, several parallels with I Peter 5:1-5 suggest those there called Elders. Even there, though, the term is apparently used in both a general (verse five) and a specific (verse one) way.

13:18. **Pray for us,** the author urges, **for we trust** (or perhaps, are persuaded) that **we have a good conscience** and are **willing** or wishing **to live honestly in all things.** Some think that the author had been criticized or suspected of evil doing by certain of his readers. Whether that is the case or not we can not tell. He simply states a request and makes a statement of good conscience. Nor do we know whom the author includes in his **we.**

19 But I beseech you the rather to do this, that I may be restored to you the sooner.

20 Now the God of peace, that brought again from the dead our Lord Jesus, that great Shepherd of the sheep, through the blood of the everlasting covenant,

---

13:19. The **rather** is better translated "abundantly" or "exceedingly," and may modify either **beseech** or **to do** or both. He strongly requests their earnest prayers, **that** he **may be restored** or reunited to them **the sooner.** It is an assumption to say that the author was in prison at this time; he could have been on a preaching tour or some other mission. All the text proves is that he was not presently with his readers but hoped to be shortly, and that he asked for their prayers to that end.

13:20. This verse and the next give the author's benediction for his readers and touch on the major points of his teaching throughout the epistle. He calls on **the God of peace,** a designation comforting for worshippers who faced persecution or even instructive discipline. As is usual in Scripture, God is described in terms of His mighty acts. He **brought again from the dead our Lord Jesus.** This is the only explicit reference in Hebrews to the resurrection of Christ, though that has been presupposed throughout the discussion, and was necessary if the sacrificial victim were to become a living high priest.

Christ is described as **that great Shepherd of the sheep.** Not only do the church leaders watch for souls under His charge (on the analogy of I Peter five) but, as the **great Shepherd,** Christ has laid down His life for the sheep (see John ten). **The blood of the everlasting covenant** is related to the resurrection, as the evident sign and seal of its merits, and to the **great Shepherd** who proved His right to the title by shedding His blood.

Of Moses and Israel it was said that God "brought them up out of the sea with the shepherd of His flock" (Isaiah 63:11; see Psalm 77:20). As Christ is counted worthy of more glory than Moses (Hebrews 3:1-6), God has brought Him up from the dead and will bring up His flock as well.

21 Make you perfect in every good work to do his
will, working in you that which is well-pleasing in his sight,
through Jesus Christ; to whom be glory for ever and ever.
Amen.

22 And I beseech you, brethren, suffer the word of
exhortation: for I have written a letter unto you in few
words.

23 Know ye that our brother Timothy is set at liberty;
with whom, if he come shortly, I will see you.

13:21. The prayer is that God, who has already raised
Christ, will now **make** the readers **perfect** or equipped **in
every good** thing for doing **his will,** and that he will be
working or doing **in** them what is **well pleasing** to Him. All
this is to be done **through Jesus Christ,** in whose name the
prayer is offered.

To whom be glory for ever and ever may apply either
to God the Father or to the Lord Jesus, and scripturally it
applies to both. Milligan says that "doctrinally it may refer
either to God or to Christ, but grammatically, it refers properly to God" in this passage. Lenski applies it to Christ
here and sees it as complementary to the description of
Christ's exalted position in chapter one.

13:22. Our author appeals to his readers to bear with his
word of exhortation, meaning the entire book. He refers to
it as **a letter,** although it is not in regular epistolary form.
He apparently had much more he would have been pleased
to write (see 5:11; 11:32), but he stops with these **few
words** which may be read in about an hour.

13:23. **Brother Timothy** had been **set at liberty,** a phrase
which might refer either to release from prison or to the
completion of a mission. **With** him our author **will see** his
readers **if** Timothy comes **shortly.** This verse is used as an
argument for the Pauline authorship of Hebrews because of
the close relationship between Paul and Timothy. We may
wish such matters were clearly revealed, but in fact they are
not, and no specific relationship is given here between the
author and Timothy. It is generally assumed, however, that
this is the Timothy of Paul's epistles and Acts, which gives

24 Salute all them that have the rule over you, and all the saints. They of Italy salute you.

25 Grace be with you all. Amen.

---

an outward time limit for the date of the book. Again, however, we are unable to learn much from the fact, for we have no information at all about an imprisonment of Timothy — if that is the meaning intended by the phrase here.

13:24. The writer sends greetings to **all** the leaders and **all the saints,** indicating that the epistle would be read in a gathered assembly of the Christians to whom it was sent (see Colossians 4:16; I Thessalonians 5:27).

They of Italy are simply "the Italians." The Greek words do not tell whether they and our author were in Italy or away from Italy at the time. All we can know from this verse is that he was in company with some Italians, wherever he was. Those who argue for a Roman destination of the epistle use this verse as evidence, as do those who argue for a Roman origin.

13:25. The epistle closes with the familiar Christian greeting. **Grace be with you all. Amen.** A suggestive discussion entitled **The Grace of God** is available from the publisher by the author of this commentary.

The subscript in some Bibles concerning the author, origin and destination of the Epistle to the Hebrews is a later addition, not part of the original text.

APPENDICES

APPENDIX I: THE OFFICIATING PRIESTHOOD

It need scarcely be said that everything connected with the priesthood was intended to be symbolical and typical — the office itself, its functions, even its dress and outward support. The fundamental design of Israel itself was to be unto Jehovah "a kingdom of priests and an holy nation" (Exodus 19:5-6). This, however, could only be realized in "the fulness of time." At the very outset there was the barrier of sin; and in order to gain admittance to the ranks of Israel, when "the sum of the children of Israel was taken after their number," every man had to give the half-shekel, which in after times became the regular Temple contribution, as "a ransom (covering) for his soul unto Jehovah" (Exodus 30:12-13). But even so Israel was sinful, and could only approach Jehovah in the way which He Himself opened, and in the manner which He appointed. Direct choice and appointment by God were the conditions alike of the priesthood, of sacrifices, feasts, and of every detail of service.

The fundamental ideas which underlay all and connected it into a harmonious whole were **reconciliation** and **mediation:** the one expressed by typically atoning sacrifices, the other by a typically intervening priesthood. Even the Hebrew term for priest **(Cohen)** denotes in its root-meaning "one who stands up for another, and mediates in his cause." For this purpose God chose the **tribe of Levi,** and out of it again the **family of Aaron,** on whom He bestowed the "priest's office as a gift" (Numbers 18:7). But the whole characteristics and the functions of the priesthood centered in the **person of the high-priest.** In accordance with their Divine "calling" (Hebrews 5:4) was the special and exceptional provision made for the support of the priesthood. Its principle was thus expressed: "I am thy part and thine inheritance among the children of Israel;" and its joyousness, when realized in its full meaning and application, found vent in such words as Psalm 16:5-6, "Jehovah is the portion of mine inheritance and of my cup: Thou maintainest my lot. The lines are fallen unto me in pleasant places; yea, I have a goodly heritage."

But there was yet another idea to be expressed by the priesthood. The object of reconciliation was **holiness**. Israel was to be "a holy nation" — reconciled through the "sprinkling of blood;" brought near to, and kept in fellowship with God by that means. The priesthood, as the representative offerers of that blood and mediators of the people, were also to show forth the "holiness" of Israel. Everyone knows how this was symbolized by the gold-plate which the high-priest wore on his forehead, and which bore the words: "Holiness unto Jehovah." But though the high-priest in this, as in every other respect, was the fullest embodiment of the functions and the object of the priesthood, the same truth was also otherwise shown forth.

The **bodily qualifications** required in the priesthood, the kind of **defilements** which would temporarily or wholly interrupt their functions, their **mode of ordination,** and even every portion, material, and color of their **distinctive dress** were all intended to express in a symbolical manner this characteristic of holiness. In all these respects there was a difference between Israel and the tribe of Levi; between the tribe of Levi and the family of Aaron; and, finally, between an ordinary priest and the high-priest, who most fully typified our Great High-priest, in whom all these symbols have found their reality.

Alfred Edersheim, **The Temple, its Ministry and Services,** pp. 60-62.

APPENDIX II: SACRIFICES: THEIR ORDER
AND THEIR MEANING

It is a curious fact, but sadly significant, that modern Judaism should declare neither sacrifices nor a Levitical priesthood to belong to the essence of the Old Testament; that, in fact, they had been foreign elements imported into it — tolerated, indeed, by Moses, but against which the prophets earnestly protested and incessantly laboured. The only arguments by which this strange statement is supported are that the Book of Deuteronomy contains merely a brief summary, not a detailed repetition, of sacrificial ordinances, and that such passages as Isaiah 1:11ff; Micah 6:6ff inveigh against sacrifices offered without real repentance or changing of mind. Yet this anti-sacrificial, or, as we may call it, anti-spiritual, tendency is really of much earlier date. For the sacrifices of the Old Testament were not merely outward observances — a sort of work-righteousness which justified the offerer by the mere fact of his obedience — since "it is not possible that the blood of bulls and of goats should take away sins" (Hebrews 10:4).

The sacrifices of the Old Testament were symbolical and typical. An outward observance without any real inward meaning is only a ceremony. But a rite which has a present spiritual meaning is a symbol; and if, besides, it also points to a future reality, conveying at the same time, by anticipation, the blessing that is yet to appear, it is a type. Thus the Old Testament sacrifices were not only symbols, nor yet merely predictions by fact (as prophecy is a prediction by word), but they already conveyed to the believing Israelite the blessing that was to flow from the future reality to which they pointed. Hence the service of the letter and the work-righteousness of the Scribes and Pharisees ran directly contrary to this hope of faith and spiritual view of sacrifices, which placed all on the level of sinners to be saved by the substitution of another, to whom they pointed.

Afterwards, when the destruction of the Temple rendered its services impossible, another and most cogent reason was added for trying to substitute other things, such as prayers, fasts, etc., in room of the sacrifices. Therefore, although none of the older Rabbis has ventured on such an assertion as that of modern Judaism, the tendency must have been increasingly in that direction. In fact, it had become a necessity — since to declare sacrifices of the essence of Judaism would have been to pronounce modern Judaism an impossibility. But thereby also the synagogue has given sentence against itself, and by disowning sacrifices has placed itself outside the pale of the Old Testament.

Every unprejudiced reader of the Bible must feel that sacrifices constitute the center of the Old Testament. Indeed, were this the place, we might argue from their universality that, along with the acknowledgment of a Divine power, the dim remembrance of a happy past, and the hope of a happier future, sacrifices belonged to the primeval traditions which mankind inherited from Paradise. To sacrifice seems as "natural" to man as to pray; the one indicates what he feels about himself, the other what he feels about God. The one means a felt need of propitiation; the other a felt sense of dependence.

The fundamental idea of sacrifice in the Old Testament is that of substitution, which again seems to imply everything else — atonement and redemption, vicarious punishment and forgiveness. The first-fruits go for the whole products; the firstlings for the flock; the redemption-money for that which cannot be offered; and the life of the sacrifice, which is in its blood (Leviticus 17:11), for the life of the sacrificer. Hence also the strict prohibition to partake of blood. Even in the "Korban" gift (Mark 7:11) or free-will offering, it is still the gift for the giver.

This idea of substitution, as introduced, adopted, and sanctioned by God Himself, is expressed by the sacrificial term rendered in our version "atonement," but which really means covering, the substitute in the acceptance of God taking the place of, and so covering, as it were, the person of the offerer. Hence the scriptural experience: "Blessed is he whose transgression is forgiven, whose sin is covered . . . unto whom the Lord imputeth not iniquity" (Psalm 32:1-2); and perhaps also the scriptural prayer: "Behold, O God, our shield, and look upon the face of Thine Anointed" (Psalm 84:9). Such sacrifices, however, necessarily pointed to a mediatorial priesthood, through whom alike they and the purified worshippers should be brought near to God, and kept in fellowship with Him. Yet these priests themselves continually changed; their own persons and services needed purification, and their sacrifices required constant renewal, since, in the nature of it, such substitution could not be perfect.

In short, all this was symbolical (of man's need, God's mercy, and His covenant), and typical, till He should come to whom it all pointed, and who had all along given reality to it; He, whose Priesthood was perfect, and who on a perfect altar brought a perfect sacrifice, once for all — a perfect Substitute, and a perfect Mediator.

*   *   *   *   *   *   *   *   *   *   *

It is deeply interesting to know that the New Testament view of sacrifices is entirely in accordance with that of the ancient Synagogue. At the threshold we here meet the principle: "There is no atonement except by blood." [For an excellent, documented treatment of Isaiah 53 in illumination of the previous statement, see **The Challenge of the Ages,** Frederick Alfred Aston, published by Research Press, 73 Hampton Road, Scarsdale, N. Y. 10583, 1971. This 24-page study proves from reliable sources that the idea of atonement was linked to the Servant of Isaiah 53 from earliest times in Jewish theology, and that only in recent centuries has that chapter been alleged as having no reference to the Messiah.] In accordance with this we quote the following from Jewish interpreters. Rashi says: "The soul of every creature is bound up in its blood; therefore I gave it to atone for the soul of man — that one soul should come and atone for the other." Similarly Aben Ezra writes: "One soul is a substitute for the other." And Moses ben Nachmann: "I gave the soul for you on the altar, that the soul of the animal should be an atonement for the soul of the man." These quotations might be almost indefinitely multiplied.

Another phase of scriptural truth appears in such Rabbinical statements as that by the imposition of hands "the offerer, as it were, puts away his sins from himself, and transfers them upon the living animal," and that "as often as any one sins with his soul, whether from haste or malice, he puts away his sin from himself, and places it upon the head of his sacrifice, and it is an atonement for him. . . ." In fact, according to Rabbinical expression, the sin-bearing animal is on that ground expressly designated as something to be rejected and abominable. The Christian reader will here be reminded of the scriptural statement: "For He has made Him to be sin for us who knew no sin, that we might be made the righteousness of God in Him."

There is yet one other phase . . . which . . . is best expressed in the following quotation, to which many similar might be added: "Properly speaking, the blood of the sinner should have been shed, and his body burned, as those of the sacrifices. But the Holy One — blessed be He! — accepted our sacrifice from us as redemption and atonement. Behold the full grace which Jehovah — blessed be He! — has shown to man! In His compassion and in the fulness of His grace He accepted the soul of the animal instead of his soul, that through it there might be an atonement." Hence also the principle, so important as an answer to the question whether the Israelites of old had understood the meaning of sacrifices. "He that brought a sacrifice required [sic] to come to the knowledge that the sacrifice was his redemption."

In view of all this, the deep-felt want so often expressed by the Synagogue [of modern times] is most touching. In the liturgy for the Day of Atonement we read: "While the altar and the sanctuary were still in their places, we were atoned for by the goats, designated by lot. But now for our guilt, if Jehovah be pleased to destroy us, He takes from our hand neither burnt-offering nor sacrifice." We add only one more out of many similar passages in the Jewish prayer-book: "We have spoken violence and rebellion; we have walked in a way that is not right. . . . Behold, our transgressions have increased upon us; they press upon us like a burden; they have gone over our heads; we have forsaken Thy commandments, which are excellent. And wherewith shall we appear before Thee, the mighty God, to atone for our transgressions, and to put away our trespasses, and to remove sin, and to magnify Thy grace? Sacrifices and offerings are no more; sin- and trespass-offerings have ceased; the blood of sacrifices is no longer sprinkled; destroyed is Thy holy house, and fallen the gates of Thy sanctuary; Thy holy city lies desolate; Thou hast slain, sent from Thy presence; they have gone, driven forth from before Thy face, the priests who have brought Thy sacrifices!" Accordingly, also, the petition frequently recurs: "Raise up for us a right Inter-cessor (that it may be true), I have found a ransom (an atonement, or covering)."

. . . Who shall make answer to this deep lament of exiled Judah? Where shall a ransom be found to take the place of their sacrifices? In their despair some appeal to the merits of the fathers or of the pious; others to their own or to Israel's sufferings, or to death, which is regarded as the last expiation. But the most melancholy exhibition, perhaps, is that of an attempted sacrifice by each pious Israelite on the eve of the Day of Atonement. Taking for males a white cock, and for females a hen, the head of the house prays . . . . Next, the head of the house swings the sacrifice round his head, saying, "This is my substitute; this is in exchange for me; this is my atonement. This cock goes into death, but may I enter into a long and happy life, and into peace!" Then he repeats this prayer three times, and lays his hands on the sacrifice which is now slain.

This offering up of an animal not sanctioned by the law, in a place, in a manner, and by hands not authorized by God, is it not a terrible phantom of Israel's dark and deary night? and does it not seem strangely to remind us of that other terrible night, when the threefold crowing of a cock awakened Peter to the fact of his denial of "the Lamb of God which taketh away the sin of the world?"

And still the cry of the Synagogue comes to us through these many centuries of past unbelief and ignorance: "Let one innocent come and make atonement for the guilty!" To which no other response can ever be made than that of the apostle: "Such an High-Priest became us, who is holy, harmless, undefiled, separate from sinners, and made higher than the heavens! (Hebrews 7:26).

Alfred Edersheim, **The Temple, its Ministry and Services**, pp. 79-82; 91-95.

APPENDIX III: SACRIFICE IN HEBREWS

. . . In connection with the term "sacrifice" we are inclined to think too narrowly of the slaying of the victim. To do so leaves out of account an act of co-equal if not of greater importance in the ritual. For this reason it is better to avail ourselves, as the author throughout does, of the verb ("to offer") which, owing to the peculiar point of view from which it regards the transaction, is precisely adapted to call to mind that which follows the death of the sacrifice. Where the author refers to the offering of Christ, he by no means restricts the range of this act to what happened on Calvary; to his view the offering was not finished there; its culminating stage lay in the self-presentation of Christ or in the presentation of His blood, as it is variously expressed, before God in heaven. Sometimes he even refers to this latter act, not as a part or the climax of the offering, but as "the offering" par excellence. And what is true of the offering is true of the "expiation." This also is not confined to the cross: Christ expiates in heaven as well as on Calvary. Evidently the process as a whole is covered by the terms, which consequently can be applied to each half of it, yet so that the second stage more clearly brings out its real significance and throws back its light upon the first. . . .

Geerhardus Vos, **Princeton Theological Review**, p. 24.

APPENDIX IV: CHRIST'S SACRIFICE
AND THE CHRISTIAN

We know that God will judge the world because He has raised Christ from the dead, and therefore all men should now repent. This is the teaching of Acts 17:30-31. But why does it follow from the resurrection of Christ that God will judge the world?

Life and death go together, as do resurrection and judgment. If a man lives we expect him to die, and if a man is raised his judgment is imminent. The pair resurrection/judgment is so intertwined that we may conceive of the time for resurrection and the time for judgment as a single brief period at the consummation of the age. This is also the biblical point of view.

Because Christ has already been raised and judged (He was acquitted of all charges of evil and pronounced blameless on the basis of His perfectly submissive and obedient life), the era has already come for all men to be raised and judged. The countdown has begun, but only God knows the number. Or, to look from another direction, we may think of God counting men as they are raised and judged. With Jesus He has already said, "Number One." Creation now waits for Him to continue the count, and, though He has presently paused, there is no reason why He may not resume at any moment.

Because Christ died to bear the sins of many, and entered God's presence to appear for us — and because His sacrifice was perfect and sufficient for all men and for all time — those who are His people in the new covenant may know that the judgment verdict is already decided in their favor. Who can condemn? It is Christ who died, and is risen again, and is even now at God's right hand making intercession for His people! His people plan to throw themselves on the mercy of the Judge and plead the blood of Christ alone, but Christ is already in heaven pleading their cause by that same perfect-life blood. Furthermore, God has judged the basis of their plea, and has rendered a favorable decision regarding it.

The determining factor in the judgment of God's people is already decided before they enter the courtroom — by the reception they gave the Son. All judgment depends on this, and the one who receives the Son in truth and holds fast to Him cannot be condemned. All sins and all good works may be set out of the picture for the moment, and we may state with full biblical assurance that judgment is summed up in the reception given (1) by God, and (2) by man, to the sacrifice of Jesus Christ which occurred once for all in history in the beginning of these last days.

The first question regards God's acceptance of the sacrifice, and the book of Hebrews answers this question with a resounding affirmation: God has already accepted the perfect offering of Christ and He will receive Christ's new-covenant people on its merits. Only the second question remains, and it involves each man individually. Will he accept this sacrifice by faith as his basis of salvation, then hold fast the confidence in Him who is author of eternal salvation to all who obey? If so, his salvation is guaranteed. But if not, that man will not be a partaker of Christ's benefits, though all the faithful covenant people surely will.

Salvation has been brought down! The choice is for each man. The perfect sacrifice has been offered and accepted. But each individual must cast away all human pride and claims, throw Himself totally upon the mercy of the Court and plead only the blood of Christ. The man who does this will not hesitate or balk in obedience to anything God has commanded him to do, but will joyfully offer himself — body, soul, and spirit — as a grateful and consecrated thank-offering, eager to do all that is asked by the One who became first his Sin-offering and, because of that, the author of his eternal salvation.

The cross of Christ touches earth and points toward heaven; its two arms are outstretched in invitation. The Lamb of God has died. Judgment has taken place already for One Man. The verdict is in. Only one question remains: Where do YOU stand? Come to the Savior! Put your faith wholly in Him! Turn from sin and self to serve Him! Speak your faith aloud — be led by it to join Christ in burial and resurrection as you obey Him in water baptism! Then serve Him gratefully, joyfully and fully so long as He gives you life! There is no other way.

APPENDIX V: THE RITUAL OF THE
DAY OF ATONEMENT

The following account of the Jewish observance
of the Day of Atonement is that of Moses ben Mai-
mon, a Jewish philosopher and codifier of the 12th
century A.D. Maimonides (as he is often called) was
born in Cordova, Spain on March 30, 1135, and he
died in Cairo, Egypt, December 13, 1204.

Maimonides set out to compile all the Jewish
traditions of past centuries in an orderly form. His
great work which emerged is known as the *Mishneh
Torah* (Repetition of the Law) or the *Yad Hahazakah*
(Strong Hand). "For systematic structure and logical
presentation" the work "has no equal in Jewish literature," according to *The Universal Jewish Encyclope-
dia.*

The account of Maimonides does not purport to
describe the Old Testament observance of the Day of
Atonement, but it is the most authoritative record
available today of the observance after Old Testament
days, including the period after Christ which saw the
writing of The Epistle to the Hebrews. He divides his
account into four sections, each further broken down
into individual *halacha*, or precepts of the rabbis.

I have eliminated all unnecessary Hebrew words,
several technical footnotes and certain of the author's
scholarly asides, but otherwise the following is as it appears in English at the end of the great commentary
by Delitzsch which is listed in my bibliography.

THE RITUAL OF THE DAY OF ATONEMENT
FIRST SECTION

Halacha 1. On the day of the fast the morning and evening sacrifice is offered just as on any other day, and also the oblation of the day, — a bull, a ram, and seven lambs, all of them burnt-offerings, and a he-goat as a sin-offering, the blood of which was sprinkled in the outer place (of the sanctuary), the flesh being eaten in the evening.

But in addition to these (regular) sacrifices, there were also offered a young bull as a sin-offering, which was consumed, and a ram as a burnt-offering, both of which the high priest had to provide out of his own means. But the ram, which was provided out of the public means . . . is that which is reckoned in **Numbers** among the sacrifices of the feast, and is called the ram of the people. Lastly, two he-goats were provided by the public means; one of which was offered as a sin-offering, and consumed by fire, and the other was to be driven away as the scapegoat.

The whole number of the sacrificial victims for this day was therefore fifteen: two daily sacrifices, one bull, two rams, and seven lambs, all burnt-offerings: in addition to these, two goats as sin-offerings, one of which was eaten in the evening, the blood being sprinkled without; the other, the blood of which was sprinkled within, was burnt: lastly, the high priest's bull as a sin-offering, which was burnt.

Halacha 2. The service as regards all the fifteen victims on this day was performed by the high priest alone, either by him who was anointed with the anointing oil [at the time of the first temple] or by him who was (merely) distinguished for the occasion by wearing the official garments [at the time of the second temple]. And if it was a Sabbath, no one but the high priest offered the Sabbath oblation. Likewise, in respect of the other ministries of this day — such as the daily fumigation and cleaning of the lamps — all was done by the high priest, who was a married man, as it is written (Leviticus 16:6), "And he shall make an atonement for himself and for his house," that is, for his wife.

Halacha 3. Seven days before the day of atonement, the high priest is removed from his own house to his chamber in the sanctuary: this is handed down from Moses our teacher. He must also for these seven days keep away from his wife; for it might happen unto her according to the custom of women, and he might then become unclean and unfit for the divine service for seven days. A deputy high priest is also to be previously appointed; so that, in case any legal hindrance set the high priest aside from the ministry, the other might act in his stead. Should any hindrance prevent the high priest from ministering before the daily morning sacrifice, or even after he had offered his own sacrifice, he that officiates in his place needs no special consecration; but his ministerial action supplies the consecration, and he begins with that act of the service at which the other left off. When the day of atonement is over, the first returns to his ministry, and the second leaves it. All the precepts of the law regarding the high priest apply to him, although in case of necessity it is valid; and if the first high priest is removed by death, the second is instituted in his place.

Halacha 4. During these seven days he is sprinkled with the ashes of a heifer, — on the third day after his separation, and on the seventh, that is, on the day of preparation for the feast of atonement; for he might unwittingly have made himself unclean. If either of these days falls upon a Sabbath, the sprinkling is omitted.

Halacha 5. During these seven days he is to exercise himself in all the performances of the service: he sprinkles the blood, takes care of the fumigation, cleanses the lamps, and brings the pieces of the daily sacrifice to the altar-fire, so that he may be accustomed to the service on the day of atonement. He has associated with him elders of the high court, who read to him, and instruct him in the ritual and ordinances of worship of the day, and address him: "My lord! high priest! Read thou with thy mouth; perhaps thou hast forgotten or never learnt this point." And on the day of preparation for the day of atonement, early in the morning, he is made to take his stand in the eastern gates; and bulls, rams, and lambs were led by in front of him, so that he might become experienced and versed in the service.

Halacha 6. During the whole of the seven days meat and drink were not withheld from him; but after nightfall, on the day of preparation for the day of atonement, he was not permitted to eat much, because food tends to make one drowsy; and he was not allowed to sleep, lest any impurity might affect him. Of course he was not allowed to eat things which might cause pollution, such as eggs, warm milk, etc.

Halacha 7. In the days of the second temple a free-thinking spirit flourished in Israel; and the Sadducees arose —may they soon disappear! — who do not believe oral teaching. They said that, on the day of atonement, the incense was to be lighted in the temple outside the veil, and that when the smoke ascended therefrom it was to be carried inside into the holiest of holies. The reason for this is, that they explain the words of Scripture (Leviticus 16:2, "For I will appear in the cloud on the mercy-seat") as referring to the clouds proceeding from the incense. But sages have learnt by tradition that the frankincense was first lighted in the holy of holies facing the ark, as it is written (Leviticus 16:13), "And he shall put the incense upon the fire before Jehovah." Now, because in the second temple they entertained the apprehension that the then existing high priest might incline to the free-thinking party, they therefore, on the preparation day for the day of atonement, conjured him, saying: "My lord! high priest! We are delegates of the high court, but thou art delegate both for us and the high court; we conjure thee by Him who causes His name to rest upon this house, we conjure thee to make no change in anything that we have said to thee." Thereupon he goes away and weeps because they had suspected him of free-thinking, and they go away and weep because they had entertained a suspicion against a person whose conduct was unknown to them; for perhaps he had nothing of the kind in his thoughts.

Halacha 8. The whole night before the day of atonement the priest sits and gives didactic expositions, that is, if he be a sage; if he be only a disciple, doctrinal expositions are addressed to him. If he be practised in reading, he reads out; if not, some one reads out to him, lest he should fall asleep. And what is it that is read from? From the holy

Scriptures. If he is disposed to fall into a slumber, the Levitical youths suddenly touch him with the middle finger, and say to him, "My lord! high priest! Stand up, and refresh thyself a little by walking on the floor, lest thou sleepest." And thus employment was found for him until the hour for slaying the victims drew near; but they did not slay them until they were certainly convinced that morning twilight had broken, lest they should slay them by night.

SECOND SECTION

Halacha 1. All sacrificial actions, as regards both the daily offerings and also the oblations, are performed by the high priest on the same day, clothed in the golden robes. The ritual peculiar to the day is, however, performed in the white robes. The service peculiar to the day consists in the dealings with the bull of the high priest and the two goats, one of which was to be the scapegoat, and in the fumigation with frankincense in the holy of holies; and all these matters were performed in the white clothing.

Halacha 2. As often as he changes his clothes, taking some off and putting others on, he must bathe himself; for it is written (Leviticus 16:23-24), "He shall put off the linen garments . . . and he shall wash his flesh with water in the holy place, and put on his garments."

The priest is to undergo five baths and ten washings of consecration on the same day. And how does this take place? Firstly, he takes off his ordinary clothes which he had on, and then, having bathed himself, stands up and dries himself; he then puts on the golden robes, and having consecrated his hands and feet, slays the daily sacrifice, performs the daily morning fumigation, cleanses the lamps, brings the pieces of the daily sacrifice to the fire on the altar, together with the meat-offering and the drink-offering, and offers the bull and the seven lambs for the feast-offering of the day. After this he consecrates his hands and his feet, puts off the golden robes, and having bathed, stands up and dries himself; he then puts on the white robes, consecrates his hands and feet, and performs the service of the day — the collective confession of sins, the drawing lots, the sprinkling of the blood of the sacrifice in the inner places, and the fumigating with frankincense in the holy of holies. He then gives up the goat to him who is to lead it away to Azazel [tradition takes Azazel to be the name of the place to which the goat was driven away], and severing the sacrificial portions from the bull and goat which were to be burnt, delivers up the rest of them to be consumed. After this he consecrates his hands and his feet, and takes off the white robes; and after bathing, he stands up and dries himself, and puts on the golden robes. He next consecrates his hands and feet, and offers the atonement-goat, which formed a part of the oblation of the day, his own ram and the ram of the people, which are burnt-offerings; and placing on the altar-fire the sacrificial portions of the bull and goat which were to be burnt, he offers the daily evening sacrifice. After that he consecrates his hands and feet, and takes off the golden robes; and after bathing, he stands and dries himself, and puts on the white robes. He consecrates his hands and feet, and entering the holiest of holies, takes therefrom the spoon and the censer. Next he consecrates his hands and feet, and takes off the white robes; and after bathing, he stands up and dries himself, and puts on the golden robes: he consecrates his hands and feet, and performs the daily evening fumigation; and after seeing to the care of the evening lights, consecrates his hands and feet; then, taking off the golden robes, he puts on his ordinary clothes, and goes out.

Halacha 3. These baths and consecrating washings were all performed in the sanctuary; for it is written, "And he shall wash his flesh with water in the holy place." The first bathing was an exception to this rule, and might be performed in any ordinary place, inasmuch as its aim was only to increase his attention; so that if he recollected any former impurity which still clung to him, he might in his thoughts give to this bathing the special purpose of cleansing himself from it. If a priest omitted the bathing on the occasion of the change of clothing, or the consecrating washing between the various clothings and acts of service, his ministry is nevertheless legally valid.

Halacha 4. If the high priest was old or sickly, some redhot iron plates were prepared on the day of preparation, which on the morrow were thrown into the water to take away the cold (as in the sanctuary none of the rabbinical prohibitions from work held good), or some hot water was mingled with the water of the bath of purification until the cold was taken from it.

Halacha 5. On any other day the high priest performed the consecrating washing of his hands and feet in the same basin as the other priests; but on this day, in conformity with his dignity, he washes them in a golden cup. On any other day the priests ascend on the eastern edge, and descend on the western edge, of the altar-stage; but on this day they go along in the middle, before the priest, both in ascending and descending, for his glorification. On any other day, he to whom the censer was entrusted shovelled up the glowing embers with a silver pan, and then poured them into a golden pan; but on this day the high priest shovelled them up with a golden pan and went with them into the temple: this was done so as not to fatigue him with an accumulation of acts of service. In the same way, the pan used every day held four **kab,** but that employed on this day held only three **kab;** and on every other day it was heavy, but to-day it was light; on every other day the handle of it was short, but to-day long, in order to make it lighter for the high priest, lest he might be wearied. On every other day there were three layers of fire placed on the altar, but to-day there were four, in order to adorn and crown the altar.

Halacha 6. In the Torah it says (Leviticus 16:17), "And he makes atonement for himself, and for his household, and for all the congregation of Israel." By this — thus have they learnt from tradition — oral confession of sins is to be understood; thou learnest accordingly from this, that on this day he makes three confessions of sins. First one for his own person, a second for his own person in connection with the rest of the priests; both are made over the bull of the atonement which is for him. And the third confession of sin for the whole of Israel is made over the goat which is to be driven away. He utters the name (of God) three times in each of these confessions.

What, then, is the tenor of his words? "O Jehovah! I have sinned, have failed in my duty, and committed wickedness before Thee. O Jehovah! Be propitiated for the sins, failings, and wickedness whereby I and my house have sinned, failed in duties, and committed wickedness before Thee; as it is written (Leviticus 16:30), 'For on that day he shall make an atonement for you to cleanse you, that ye may be clean from all your sins before Jehovah.' " Consequently he uttered three times the name of God, and the same in the other two confessions; and when he casts the lot for the atoning goat, he says, "A sin-offering to Jehovah." Thus on this day he utters the name of God ten times, and utters it every time as it is written, that is, the full name of God. In earlier times he raised his voice at the name of God; but an abuse of this practice crept in, and he spake it in a subdued voice, and allowed it to die away into a kind of singing, so that it was not audible even to his fellow-priests.

Halacha 7. All, both priests and people, who stood in the forecourt, so soon as they heard the full name of God proceed from the high priest in holiness and purity, knelt down, and, casting themselves prostrate on their faces, called out, "Praised be the name of the glory of His kingdom for all eternity!" for it is written (Deuteronomy 32:3), "Because I utter the name of the Lord, ascribe ye honour to our God." In all three confessions he endeavoured to finish speaking the name of God simultaneously with the words of praise, and then he spake to them, "Be ye purified." The whole day is valid according to the law for the confession of sins for the day of atonement, and also for the confession of sins over the bulls which were to be burnt.

THIRD SECTION

Halacha 1. On one of the two lots was written, "For Jehovah;" and on the other, "For Azazel." It was permissible to use any material for them, either wood, stone, or metal. It was not, however, allowed for one to be large and the other small, one of silver and another of gold; but they must be both alike: they used to be of wood, and in the second temple they were made of gold. The two lots were to be thrown into one and the same vessel, in which there was room for both hands; yet so that the two hands were pressed together, so that he could not choose one of the two lots. This vessel possessed no sacred attribute; it was made of wood, and was called **qalapi.**

Halacha 2. Where is the lot cast? On the eastern side of the fore-court, on the north of the altar, the urn was put down, and the two goats were placed by it, with their faces turned to the west, and their backs to the east. The high priest now approaches, having the consecrating priest on his right, and the chief of the ministering priestly family on his left; and the two goats stand before his face, the one on his right, the other on his left.

Halacha 3. He now dips his hands hastily into the urn, and draws out the lots, one in each hand, in the name of the two goats, and then opens his hands. If that for Jehovah has been brought out in the right hand, the consecrating priest says: "My lord! high priest! Elevate thy right hand!" If, however it is brought out in the left hand, the chief of the ministering priestly family says to him: "My lord! high priest! Elevate thy left hand!" He now places the two lots on the goats, that in his right hand on the goat on his right, and that in his left hand on the goat on his left; nevertheless, if he does not lay the lots upon them, the whole matter is not prejudiced, only he has not so fully completed the prescribed action. For the laying on is a command which is not a necessary condition; but the drawing of the lots is, on the contrary, a necessary condition, although it is not an act of divine service. Therefore this laying on is valid, if done by one not a priest; but the drawing the lots out of the urn would be invalid if thus performed.

Halacha 4. And he ties a scarlet stripe, two **selas** in weight, on the head of the goat which is to be driven away, and places it opposite to the door at which it is to go out; but the goat which is to be slain (he binds a stripe) around its neck, and then slays the "bull of atonement which is for him," and (after that) the goat on which the lot has fallen "for Jehovah."

Halacha 5. And he brings their blood into the temple, and from the blood of the two he makes forty-three sprinklings; the blood of the bull he sprinkles eight times in the holiest of holies, between the poles of the ark, within a hand's breadth of the mercy-seat. For it is written, "He shall sprinkle it before the mercy-seat," etc.: he sprinkles it therefore, once above, and seven times beneath. They have learned by tradition that in the Scripture term "seven times" the first sprinkling was not to be included; and therefore he reckons, "once and one, once and two, once and three, once and four, once and five, once and six, once and seven."

And why does he reckon thus? Lest by error the first sprinkling should be reckoned among the seven. Then he sprinkles the blood of the goat between the poles of the ark, once above, and seven times below, and reckons in the same way as with the blood of the bull. Next he sprinkles the blood of the bull eight times in the temple on the veil, once above, and seven times below: for it is written with regard to the blood of the bull, "On the mercy-seat, and before the mercy-seat;" and he reckons in the same way as he did inside. Then he sprinkles again the blood of the goat eight times on the veil, once above, and seven times below: for it is said with regard to the blood of the goat, "He shall do with its blood as he did with the blood of the bull;" and he reckons in the same way as he did within. In all these sprinklings he endeavours not to sprinkle above or below, but does it like one who is in the act of scourging. Next he mixes the two bloods, the blood of the bull and the blood of the goat, and sprinkles it four times on the four horns of the golden altar in the temple, and seven times on the middle of this altar.

Halacha 6. In all these forty-three sprinklings he dips his finger in the blood for each sprinkling separately: one dipping is not sufficient for two sprinklings. The remainder of the blood he pours out on the ground to the west of the outer altar.

Halacha 7. He then delivers over the living goat into the hands of a man who stands by ready to lead it into the wilderness. In a legal point of view, any one is fitted for leading it away; but the high priests have made a rule, not to allow any Israelite [that is, no one who was not of the tribe of Levi] to lead it away. And tents were set up from Jerusalem to the edge of the wilderness, in which one or several men abode over the day, so as to be able to accompany the man conducting the goat from one tent to another. At each tent it was said to him, "Here is food, and here is water!" And if he was exhausted, and it was necessary for him to eat, he might do so; yet this was never the case. The people at the last tent remained standing at the end of the Sabbath-limit, and surveyed his action from afar. And what did he do? He divided into two the scarlet stripes on the horns of the goat: one-half of the band was placed on the rock, and the other half between the two horns of the goat, which he then pushed backwards, so that tumbling over it rolled down, and all its limbs were smashed to pieces ere it reached a point half-way down the hill. He that led the goat now goes and sits down in the last tent until it is night. Watch-towers were set up, and signals displayed, in order that it should be known when the goat had reached the wilderness.

After he (the high priest) has delivered over the goat into the hands of him who was to lead him away, he turns to the bull and the goat whose blood he had sprinkled within; and cutting them up, and taking therefrom the sacrificial portions, which he places in a vessel in order to take them to the fire on the altar, he cuts up the rest of the flesh into great pieces, all connected with one another, without severing them, and delivers them up into the hands of others to take them away to the place of burning, where they were cut in pieces still in the skin. . . .

Halacha 8.   As soon as the goat had reached the wilderness, the priest went out into the woman's division of the fore-court in order to read from the Torah; and whilst he was reading, the bull and the goat were burnt in the place of ashes. Whoever, then, saw the high priest whilst he was reading, could not witness the burning of the bull and the goat. The latter operation could be performed by any common man.

Halacha 9.   This reading is not a performance of divine worship; so he can read either in his own ordinary white garments or in the high-priestly white robes, just as he pleases: for he is allowed to make use of the priestly robes at other times than those of service.

Halacha 10.   And what were the circumstances attending the reading? He sits in the woman's division of the fore-court, and all the people stand in front of him. The minister of the synagogue takes the book of the Torah, and gives it to the ruler of the synagogue, who gives it to the consecrating priest: the consecrating priest gives it to the high priest, who receives it standing up; and standing up he reads . . . (Leviticus 16) and . . . (Leviticus 23:27) . . . . He then rolls up the Torah, and, placing it in his lap, says, "More is here written than that which I have read to you," and recites to them from memory the section . . . in **Numbers** up to the end of the division. And why does he not read the latter portion out of another roll? Because the same man must not read out of two rolls (one after the other), lest he should cast suspicion on the first.

Halacha 11. Before and after the reading he pronounces the benediction in the way in which it is done in the synagogue, but adding the following seven benedictions: "Be well pleased, Jehovah, our God," etc.; "We confess to Thee," etc.; "Forgive us, our Father, for we have sinned," etc. With these he pronounces the concluding formula: "Thou are praised, Jehovah, Thou that pardonest with mercy the sins of Thy people Israel."

These three benedictions are the normal ones. He then pronounces a benediction for the sanctuary separately, with the purport that the sanctuary might continue, and that God would abide therein, with the concluding formula: "Praised art thou, Jehovah, Thou that art enthroned on Zion." Also a separate benediction for Israel, with the purport that the Lord would help Israel, and that the royalty might not depart from it, with the concluding formula: "Praised art Thou, Jehovah, that Thou choosest Israel." Then for the priests a separate benediction, with the purport that God would accept their actions and ministry graciously, and would bless them, with the concluding formula: "Praised art Thou, Jehovah, Thou that sanctifiest the priests." Finally he offers prayer, devotion, singing, and supplications, according as he is practised therein, and concludes: "Help, O Jehovah, Thy people Israel, for Thy people needs Thy help. Praised art Thou, Jehovah, Thou that hearest prayer."

FOURTH SECTION

Halacha 1. The successive order of all the actions of this day was as follows: — About midnight they cast lots for the carrying away of the ashes, duly prepared the altar-fire, and took the ashes from the altar, following entirely the usual mode of procedure in the order we have already described, until they came to slaying the daily sacrifice. When they were about to slay the daily sacrifice, a cloth of linen was spread between the high priest and the people. And why of linen? In order that he may perceive that the service of the day is to be performed in linen robes. He now takes off his ordinary clothes, bathes himself, and puts on the golden robes. After consecrating his hands and feet, he cuts through the greatest part of the two neck-pipes of the daily offering; and leaving to another the completion of the act of slaying, catches the blood, and sprinkles it upon the altar according to precept. After this, he goes into the temple and looks to the early fumigation with frankincense, cleanses the lamps, and places on the altar-fire the pieces of the daily offering, and also the meat-offering and drink-offering, in the same order as in the daily sacrifice of any other day, as already described. After the daily sacrifice he offers the bull and the seven lambs as the feast-offerings of the day, and consecrating his hands and feet, takes off the golden robes; then having bathed himself, he puts on the white robes, and, consecrating his hands and his feet, approaches his own bull. The latter is placed between the porch and the altar, the head towards the south and the face towards the west; the priest stands on the east of it with his face turned towards the west, and laying both hands on the head of the bull, pronounces the confession of sins. And thus he speaks: "O Jehovah, I have sinned, committed transgressions, and wickedness in which I have sinned, transgressed, and done wickedly before Thee, I and my house; as it is thus written in the law of Moses Thy servant: 'He shall make atonement for you to cleanse you, that ye may be cleansed from all your sins before Jehovah.' "

Then he casts lots over the two goats, fastens a scarlet stripe on the head of the goat which was to be sent away, and places it before the door at which it was to go out. On the head of the goat which was to be slain (he fastened a band) in the region of the neck; and approaching his own bull a second time, lays his hands upon his head, and pronounces a second confession of sins. And thus he spake: "O Jehovah, I have sinned, transgressed, and committed

wickedness before Thee, I and my house, and the sons of
Aaron, the people of Thy sacred things. O Jehovah, let
atonement be made for the sins, transgressions, and wickedness whereby I have sinned, transgressed, and done wickedly before Thee, I and my house, and the sons of Aaron,
the people of Thy holy things; as it as written in the law
of Moses Thy servant: 'For on this day,' " etc. Hereupon he
slays the bull, and catching the blood, gives it to some one,
who shakes it, lest it should coagulate; then, placing it on the
fourth row of pavement outwards from the temple, he takes
the incense-pan and shovels into it the fiery embers from
the altar, those indeed which lie to the western side; as it is
written, "from the altar of Jehovah." He then descends
and places them on the pavement in the fore-court; and there
is brought to him out of the utensil-chamber the ladle and
a vessel full of the very finest frankincense: of this he takes
two handfuls, neither levelled nor heaped up, but just handfuls, whether he be large or small in his bodily proportions,
and places them in the ladle.

We have already explained elsewhere, that, as regarded
the blood of the sanctuary and the rest of the ministerial
actions, the use of the left hand caused a legal invalidity;
therefore, in conformity with this, he would have carried
the incense-pan in his left hand, and the ladle with the frankincense in his right hand. But nevertheless, on account of
the heavy burden of the incense-pan, and because, moreover, it was hot, he could not carry it in his left hand as far
as the ark: he therefore took the incense-pan in his right
hand, and the ladle with the frankincense in his left, and
passed through the temple till he reached the holy of holies.
If he found the veil fastened up, he entered the holy of
holies, until he came to the ark. When he reached the ark
he placed the incense-pan between the two poles — in the
second temple, where there was no ark, he placed it on the
"foundation stone" — and, taking the ladle by its edge either in the tips of his fingers or his teeth, he empties the
frankincense with his thumb into his hands until they are
as full of it as they were before; and this is one of the
severest ministerial duties in the sanctuary: he then with
his hand pours the frankincense in heaps upon the charcoal
on the inner side of the pan [that is, on the side farthest
from him], so that the fumigation may be closest to the

ark, and removed away from his face, lest he might be burnt. He now waits there until the temple is full of the incense and then goes out, walking backwards step by step, his face turned to the sanctuary, and his back to the temple, until he came outside the veil. After coming out he prays there but a brief prayer, lest he might make the people anxious whether he had not met with his death in the temple. And thus he prayed: "Jehovah, our God, let it be Thy will, if this year should be a hot year, that it may be blessed with rain; may the sceptre not depart from the house of Judah; may Thy people, the house of Israel, never be wanting in support, and let not the prayer of those journeying come before thee" [who pray for dry weather whilst the land is in need of rain].

Halacha 2. During the time of the incense-burning in the holiest of holies, the whole of the people kept away from the temple only: they had not to avoid the interval between the porch and the altar. For the latter is done only in the daily fumigation in the temple, and during the blood-sprinkling there. Then he takes the blood of the bull from him who is shaking it, and going with it into the holiest of holies, sprinkles it there eight times between the poles of the ark; he then goes out and places it in the temple, on the golden pedestal which stands there. In the next place, going out of the temple, he slays the goat, and, catching its blood, carries it into the holiest of holies; there he sprinkles it eight times between the poles of the ark, and going out, places it on the second golden pedestal standing in the temple. Then he takes the blood of the bull down from the pedestal, and sprinkles it eight times on the veil opposite the ark; and putting down the blood of the bull, he takes down the blood of the goat, and sprinkles it eight times on the veil opposite the ark. After that he pours the blood of the bull amongst that of the goat, and empties it all into the basin in which the blood of the bull had been, so that they are well mixed; and standing within the golden altar, between the altar and the candlesticks, he begins to sprinkle the mixed blood on the horns of the golden altar, going round the same outside the horns, commencing with the north-eastern horn, then going to the north-western, then to the south-western, and then to the south-eastern. All the sprinklings are made in an upward direction, the last excepted, which is made freely, and in a downward direction, so that his robes may not be soiled; then he shovels aside the charcoal and ashes on the golden altar, until the gold of it is visible, and sprinkles the mixed blood on the altar now laid bare seven times on the southern side, on the spot where the horns of the altar end; he now goes out and pours the rest of the blood on the ground to the west of the outer altar.

Then he approaches the goat which is to be given away, and, placing both hands on its head, pronounces a confession of sins. And he speaks thus: "O Jehovah, Thy people the house of Israel hath sinned, transgressed, and committed wickedness before Thee. O Jehovah, let atonement be made for the sins, transgressions, and the wickedness whereby Thy people the house of Israel hath sinned, transgressed, and committed wickedness before Thee; as it is written in the law of Moses Thy servant: 'For on this day He will make atonement,' " etc.

After this he sends the goat away into the wilderness; and taking out the sacrificial portions of the bull and the goat, the blood of which he had sprinkled inside, and placing them in a vessel, he sends the remainder of them to the place of ashes to be burnt, and goes out into the woman's division of the fore-court, and there reads, after the goat had reached the wilderness. Then he performs a consecrating washing, and having taken off the golden robes, bathes himself, puts on the white robes, and consecrates his hands and his feet; next he sacrifices the goat, the blood of which is sprinkled without, and forms a part of the regular feast-offering of the day, and offers his own ram and the ram of the people, as it is written: "And he shall go out and offer his burnt-offering and the burnt-offering of the people." And having brought to the altar-fire the sacrificial portions of the bull and goat which are to be burnt, he offers the daily evening sacrifice. Then he consecrates his hands and feet, takes off the golden robes, bathes himself, puts on the white robes, performs the consecrating washing, and, entering the holiest of holies, brings out the spoon and the pan. After this he performs the consecrating washing, takes off the white robes, bathes himself, puts on the golden robes, performs the consecrating washing, fumigates with the evening incense, and gives his attention to the evening lights, just as on other days. Then he consecrates his hands and his feet, takes off the golden robes, and, putting on his ordinary clothes, withdraws to his own house. All the people accompany him to his house, and he holds a festival to celebrate his having come successfully out of the sanctuary.

14.3.74

SELECTED BIBLIOGRAPHY

COMMENTARIES AND SPECIAL STUDIES
OF HEBREWS

Archer, Gleason L., Jr. *The Epistle to the Hebrews: A Study Manual.* Grand Rapids: Baker Book House, 1957.

Barrett, C. K. "The Eschatology of the Epistle to the Hebrews," *The Background of the New Testament and Its Eschatology* (Hon. C. H. Dodd), edited by W. D. Davies and D. Daube. Cambridge: The University Press, 1956.

Bruce, F. F. *The Epistle to the Hebrews: The New International Commentary.* Grand Rapids: William B. Eerdmans Publishing Company, 1964.

Clark, Adam. *Commentary and Notes.* Volume 6. Nashville: Abingdon Press, no date.

Delitzsch, Franz. *Commentary on the Epistle to the Hebrews: Clark's Foreign Theological Library.* Two volumes. Edinburgh: T. & T. Clark, 1887.

Dods, Marcus. *The Epistle to the Hebrews: The Expositor's Greek Testament.* Volume 4. Grand Rapids: William B. Eerdmans Publishing Company, 1964.

Filson, Floyd V. *"Yesterday": A Study of Hebrews in the Light of Chapter 13* (Studies in Biblical Theology, Second series, 4). Naperville, Illinois: Alec R. Allenson, Inc., 1967.

Johnson, B. W. *The People's New Testament With Notes.* Nashville: Gospel Advocate Company, no date.

Kistemaker, Simon. *The Psalm Citations in the Epistle to the Hebrews.* Amsterdam: Wed. G. Van Soest N.V., 1961.

Lenski, R. C. H. *The Interpretation of the Epistle to the Hebrews.* Columbus, Ohio: The Wartburg Press, 1946.

Milligan, Robert. *Epistle to the Hebrews: The New Testament Commentary.* Nashville: Gospel Advocate Company, 1963.

Nairne, Alexander. *The Epistle to the Hebrews.* Cambridge: The University Press, 1921.

Robinson, Theodore H. *The Epistle to the Hebrews: The Moffatt New Testament Commentary.* New York: Harper and Brothers Publishers, no date.

Rotherham, Joseph B. *Studies in the Epistle to the Hebrews.* Joplin, Missouri: College Press, Reprint edition, no date.

Woods, Clyde. "Eschatological Motifs in the Epistle to the Hebrews," *The Last Things* (Hon. W. B. West, Jr.), edited by Jack P. Lewis. Austin: Sweet Publishing Company, 1972.

PERIODICALS

Adams, J. Clifford, "Exegesis of Heb VI. 1f," *New Testament Studies,* 13 (March, 1967), 378-385.

Brooks, Walter Edward, "The Perpetuity of Christ's Sacrifice in the Epistle to the Hebrews," *Journal of Biblical Literature,* 89 (June, 1970), 205-214.

Bruce, F. F. "Recent Contributions to the Understanding of Hebrews," *The Expository Times,* 80 (September, 1969), 260-264.

——————. "The Kerygma of Hebrews," *Interpretation,* 23 (January, 1969), 3-19.

Higgins, A. J. B. "The Priestly Messiah," *New Testament Studies,* 13 (March, 1967), 211-239.

Howard, George. "Hebrews and the Old Testament Quotations," *Novum Testamentum,* 10 (February - March, 1968), 208-216.

Huxhold, Harry N. "Faith in the Epistle to the Hebrews," *Concordia Theological Monthly,* 38 (October, 1967), 657-661.

Most, William G. "A Biblical Theology of Redemption in a Covenant Framework," *Catholic Biblical Quarterly*, 29 (January, 1967), 1-19.

Stewart, R. A. "The Sinless High-Priest," *New Testament Studies*, 14 (January, 1967), 126-135.

Stott, Wilfrid, "The Conception of 'Offering' in the Epistle to the Hebrews," *New Testament Studies*, 9 (January, 1962), 62-67.

Swetnam, James. "A Suggested Interpretation of Hebrews 9:15-18," *Catholic Biblical Quarterly*, 27 (April, 1965), 373-390.

Vos, Geerhardus, "Hebrews, the Epistle of the Diatheke," *Princeton Theological Review*, 13 (1915), 587-632; 14 (1916), 1-61.

OTHER BOOKS

Arndt, William F. and F. Wilbur Gingrich (editors). *A Greek-English Lexicon of the New Testament and Other Early Christian Literature.* Chicago: The University of Chicago Press, 1963.

Berkouwer, G. C. *The Person of Christ.* Translated from the Dutch by John Vriend. Grand Rapids: William B. Eerdmans Publishing Company, 1969.

Bernard, Thomas Dehany. *The Progress of Doctrine in the New Testament.* New York: American Tract Society, 1907.

Cullmann, Oscar. *The Christology of the New Testament.* London: SCM Press, Ltd., 1963.

Dix, Gregory. *Jew and Greek.* London: Dacre Press, 1967.

Edersheim, A. *The Temple, Its Ministry and Services.* New York: Fleming H. Revell Company, no date.

Hillers, Delbert R. *Covenant: The History of a Biblical Idea.* Baltimore: The Johns Hopkins Press, 1969.

Jocz, Jakob. *The Covenant.* Grand Rapids: William B. Eerdmans Publishing Company, 1968.

Kittel, Rudolf (editor). *Biblia Hebraica* [The Hebrew Old Testament]. Stuttgart: Wurttembergische Bibelanstalt, 1966.

Moulton, James Hope and George Milligan. *The Vocabulary of the Greek Testament Illustrated from the Papyri and Other Non-Literary Sources.* London: Hodder and Stoughton, 1963.

Philips, A. Th. (translator). *Prayer Book for the Day of Atonement.* New York: Hebrew Publishing Company, 1931.

Rahlfs, Alfred (editor). *Septuaginta* [The Greek Old Testament]. Stuttgart: Wurttembergische Bibelanstalt, 1962.

Schweizer, Eduard. *Church Order in the New Testament: Studies in Biblical Theology.* London: SCM Press, Ltd., 1961.

Smith, J. B. *Greek-English Concordance to the New Testament.* Scottdale, Pennsylvania: Herald Press, 1955.

Stalker, James. *The Atonement.* New York: A. C. Armstrong and Son, 1909.

Thayer, Joseph Henry (editor). *Greek-English Lexicon of the New Testament.* Grand Rapids: Zondervan Publishing House, 1963.

Theological Dictionary of the New Testament. Edited by Gerhard Kittel, translated by G. W. Bromiley. Six volumes. Grand Rapids: William B. Eerdmans Publishing Company, 1964-1968.

Wright, G. Ernest. *God Who Acts: Studies in Biblical Theology.* London: SCM Press, Ltd., 1969.

INDICES

I. BIBLICAL CITATIONS OUTSIDE HEBREWS
A. Old Testament

B. New Testament

II. APOCRYPHA, PSEUDEPIGRAPHA, HELLENISTIC WRITERS

III. APOSTOLIC FATHERS